Jesus Heals

Devotional

Elisa,

Happy birthday!!
You are fearfully +
wonderfully made.
by Psalm 139:14

Mary Teresa Fulp

Love, Aunt Mary
♡

Dedication

This devotional is dedicated to Jesus.

Thank you, Jesus, for giving me the words to express to others how beautiful, wide and deep your love is for them.

I am so thankful for the love that Jesus provides during the intimate alone time with just Him, as well as who He sends into my life to fellowship with. I am thankful that God answers my prayers in unexpected ways and that He loves me enough to continue to prune and prepare my heart to be more like Jesus.

I was walking through another heartbreaking season as I wrote this devotional. I have learned that you can be both completely heartbroken and full of hope at the same time. I had to dig deep to truly believe in His healing power in order to surrender the pen to Him, so that He could work through me to write the messages in this book.

"Heal me, Lord, and I will be healed; save me and I will be saved, for you are the one I praise." – Jeremiah 17:14

"'But I will restore you to health and heal your wounds,' declares the Lord." – Jeremiah 30:17

"'I have seen their ways, but I will heal them; I will guide them and restore comfort to Israel's mourners, creating praise on their lips. Peace, peace, to those far and near,' says the Lord. 'And I will heal them.'" – Isaiah 57:18-19

"He gives strength to the weary and increases the power of the weak." – Isaiah 40:29

"He sent out his word and healed them; he rescued them from the grave. Let them give thanks to the Lord for his unfailing love and his wonderful deeds for mankind." – Psalms 107:20-21

"He heals the brokenhearted and binds up their wounds." – Psalm 147:3

"Jesus went through all the towns and villages, teaching in their synagogues, proclaiming the good news of the kingdom and healing every disease and sickness." – Matthew 9:35

"He said to her, 'Daughter, your faith has healed you. Go in peace and be freed from your suffering.'" – Mark 5:34

"Lord my God, I called to you for help and you healed me." – Psalm 30:2

Contents

Show me where You need me to go 1

Take one step of faith at a time 4

Living on a deeper level 6

Give it to God 8

Be Uniquely You 10

Trust God 12

Love Permits Pain 14

He Fights for Us 16

Daily Habits for God's Plan 18

Live by Faith 20

Serve Others 22

Love others 24

In My Weakness, He Is strong 26

Your Breakthrough is Coming 29

Choose a Positive Attitude 31

Be Impeccable with Your Word 33

God Knows and Cares 36

Speak the Truth in Love 39

Do the Right Thing 41

Walk in the Spirit 43

Pray and Seek His Face 45

Focus on the Good 47

Choose to Be Happy 50

Learn to Receive 53

Arise and Shine.. 55

A Holy Spirit Makeover... 57

Path to Prosperity... 60

God Has Planted You 62

The Steps of Faith 64

Call Out to Jesus 66

Let God Heal Your Heart.. 68

Purify My Heart 70

Reflect His Image.. 72

God Meets Us in Our Sorrow.................................. 74

Delight in the Lord.. 76

Taken Aside by Jesus... 78

Live out the Love of God 80

Take Me into the Deep 83

Ask God for Big Things.. 85

Start Your Day with God 87

Start with the Truth 89

Lean on Him 92

You Are Chosen 94

Speak the Word.. 97

Wait in Gratitude... 99

The Anointing Lives in You.................................... 101

Go the Extra Mile... 103

Integrity Matters.. 105

Slow Down... 107

Live Victoriously 109

His Deepest Truths 111

His Purpose... 113

Unleash Your Gift... 115

Trust in Him 117

In the Darkness.. 119

Shine Bright 121

In the Morning 123

Be Positive 125

Be You... 127

Let God Fill Your Heart...................................... 130

Make the Most of Your Gift 132

Be Present with People 134

Be Christ's Image Bearer 136

Our Battles are His.. 139

You Will Succeed 142

Please God, Not People..................................... 144

Rise up and Conquer 147

Steadfast Faith.. 149

Let Them Judge & Criticize You......................... 151

Jesus Was Persecuted by the Crowd 154

He Gently Whispers... 156

Sow in Faith 159

Encourage Yourself 161

Heartfelt Prayer 163

Trust the Season You're in 165

Live with Integrity... 168

Be the Change 170

Pray Without Ceasing 172

I Am Who He Says I Am 174

New and Sharp.. 177

Be Still and Know.. 179

Seek Wisdom & Discernment............................ 181

Put on Love.. 184

Enjoy Today 187

People Will Come Against You.. 189

Lift Others Up 191

The Spirit Works for Us... 193

You Are God's Masterpiece 196

Desires of Your Heart.. 198

Joyful Spirit... 201

You Are Called 203

Your Word Lights My Path 205

Experience His Peace... 207

God Chose You 210

Hold Your Peace.. 213

Armor Up... 215

Love Like Jesus... 218

He Is Working 220

Celebrate Often 222

He Is at Work Within Us 224

Find Your Purpose 227

Listen to His Voice, His Gentle Whisper............................ 230

He Knows What Is Best for Me 234

It Comes from Within 237

Be Filled with the Spirit 239

Be Rooted and Established in Love................................... 242

Mess to Masterpiece.. 245

Wait on Him... 248

Look Out for Others... 250

He Lives in You... 252

Feed Your Faith... 254

Trials Develop Us 257

He Is My Steadfast Companion 260

He Showers Abundant Blessings upon Me 262

Wisdom Without Hypocrisy 265

He Will Provide 268

Be More Like Jesus 271

Put God First 273

Build Others up 275

Wash Your Face 277

Time with Him 280

A Fierce Storm Will Transform 282

Walk in Peace 284

Be Fiercely Authentic 286

Take the Next Step 288

Trials Are Necessary 290

You Have Found Favor 292

Choose Faith 295

Say His Name, Speak His Word 298

Acknowledgements 301

Show me where You need me to go

The Lord had said to Abram, "Go from your country, your people, and your father's household to the land I will show you." – Genesis 12:1

Are you in a place where you need direction to know what to do next? Ask God to show you where He needs you to go and what He needs you to do. He will reveal the next step at just the right time if you seek His guidance and remain centered in Him. I begin my day by sitting quietly in His presence. I read scripture and let Him speak directly to me through it. I meditate on His word to truly understand what He is saying so that it settles deeply into my heart and mind as a seed that will grow in time.

Reflect:

What is He saying to you today? What has settled deeply into your heart and mind as you spend time meditating on and reflecting on His word?

Pray:

Heavenly Father, thank you for showing me where You need me to go. Thank you for being patient with me as I learn to listen to Your voice. I ask today that You guide me to the place that You have prepared for me to go and that my trust in You does not waiver when the path appears uncertain and dark. I place my trust in You to lead me, even when I can't see or feel Your presence. I know You are working and I place my faith in You. In Jesus' name. I pray. Amen.

Declare:

I am confident the LORD will show me where He needs me to go. I believe He is guiding me to my amazing destiny in this very moment.

I am thankful for...

_____

_____

_____

_____

_____

Prayer Requests...

_____

_____

_____

_____

_____

What is God's Word saying to you today?...

_____

_____

_____

_____

_____

_____

Take one step of faith at a time

He said to them, "Because of your little faith. For truly, I say to you, if you have faith like a grain of mustard seed, you will say to this mountain, 'Move from here to there,' and it will move, and nothing will be impossible for you." - Matthew 17:20-21

My job is to follow Him, one step of faith at a time, holding every decision up to Him in thanksgiving and prayer. I have confidence knowing He lives in me and provides me with direction as I seek Him and trust my God-given intuition throughout the day. He is with me at all times and is there to guide me in the big and small, in the ordinary and in the extraordinary.

Reflect:

God, where do You want me to go? How will I know it's time to go? What do You want me to do today?

Pray:

Heavenly Father, thank you for guiding me and growing me in You. I want to live my life through Your highest purpose. I know Your will is what's best for me. I ask that You continue to show me where You need me to go. I thank You for loving and guiding me each day. Thank you Jesus, for doing a good work in me. I want to love like You. In Jesus' name, I pray. Amen.

Declare:

I am confident that the steps I take are ordered by God. My faith is in Him to do the things that seem impossible in my life.

I am thankful for...

_____

_____

_____

_____

_____

Prayer Requests...

_____

_____

_____

_____

_____

What is God's Word saying to you today?...

_____

_____

_____

_____

_____

_____

Living on a deeper level

"So then they that are in the flesh cannot please God."
- Romans 8:8

God cares about us and wants to take care of our every need. He wants greater things for us than we can possibly want for ourselves. He wants us to abandon the flesh in order to live on a deeper level. The only level that will truly satisfy our soul is the spirit level. God's presence is greater than our problems, and His purpose is greater than our pain. We can access His presence when we are in touch with the Holy Spirit who dwells within us.

Reflect:

In what ways are you being called to live on a deeper level? How would it benefit you to move from the shallow into the deep? What does that mean to you personally?

Pray:

Heavenly Father, I want a deeper, more intimate relationship with You. I know that I will need to do my part to make that happen. I ask You to help me live less in the flesh and more in the Spirit with You. In Jesus' name, I pray. Amen.

Declare:

I am connected to, God, the ultimate source who meets all of my needs. He dwells within me and gives me the wisdom, courage, and strength I need to face anything that comes my way.

I am thankful for...

_____

_____

_____

_____

_____

Prayer Requests...

_____

_____

_____

_____

_____

What is God's Word saying to you today?...

_____

_____

_____

_____

_____

_____

Give it to God

"Casting the whole of your care, all your anxieties, all your worries, all your concerns, once and for all, on Him, for He cares for you affectionately and cares about you watchfully."
- 1 Peter 5:7

In order to be our best selves, we must continually commit and surrender ourselves to God. God intervenes on our behalf when we commit our situations to Him. Commit to the Lord anything you are tempted to worry or be concerned about.

Reflect:

How can I commit my worries to God and truly leave them with Him?

Pray:

Heavenly Father, I believe You are worthy to be trusted with every situation in my life. I pray that I become better at turning to You at all times, especially during the times when I need You most. I don't want to carry burdens on my own when I know You are here to be my strength in all situations. Today, I pray for less of me and more of You. In Jesus' name, Amen.

Declare:

I am loved by the One who loves best. I can do all things in and through Him.

I am thankful for...

_____

_____

_____

_____

_____

Prayer Requests...

_____

_____

_____

_____

_____

What is God's Word saying to you today?...

_____

_____

_____

_____

_____

_____

Be Uniquely You

"And even the very hairs of your head are all numbered."
- Matthew 10:30

Find out what makes you unique, and be the best you can possibly be by embracing who you are without limits. God wants us to fit into His design, not someone else's limiting image of who they think we should be or who they think we are. You are uniquely and wonderfully made. Embrace the real you and live in your highest purpose.

Reflect:

Why did the Lord choose you? What makes you uniquely wonderful?

Pray:

Heavenly Father, this world has a way of minimizing who You created us to be in Your image. I pray that You help me take the brave steps that I need to take to live in my highest purpose as the uniquely wonderful child of Yours that You created me to be, before the world got a hold of me. In Jesus' name, I pray. Amen.

Declare:

I am uniquely made in God's image. I choose to take brave steps to live as my most authentic and loving self.

I am thankful for...

_____

_____

_____

_____

_____

Prayer Requests...

_____

_____

_____

_____

_____

What is God's Word saying to you today?...

_____

_____

_____

_____

_____

_____

Trust God

"But Jesus often withdrew to lonely places and prayed."
- Luke 5:16

Embrace alone time. Don't avoid the lonely, quiet times or places. I've avoided them all too often by trying to fill my time with things to do so I wouldn't have to face my inner self. What I've learned, the hard way, is that when I do this, I am slowing down the growth process and limiting what God can do in my life. If I trust in and spend time alone with Him, He can go to work on the inward parts of me. We need to set aside time to let our minds get quiet enough to be alone with Him in order for us to hear His voice above the noise of the world.

Reflect:

Are you avoiding or embracing alone time with God? How do you know?

Pray:

Heavenly Father, I desire a deeper relationship with You. I am thankful for the times You've provided me time in lonely places, so that I can heal and grow in relationship with You. You are my source, and I am thankful for all that I am in and through You. I pray for a relationship with You that is alive and growing throughout life. In Jesus' Name, I pray. Amen.

Declare:

I am not afraid of alone time. I am grateful to know that I am never truly alone because Jesus is always with me.

I am thankful for...

_____

_____

_____

_____

_____

Prayer Requests...

_____

_____

_____

_____

_____

What is God's Word saying to you today?...

_____

_____

_____

_____

_____

_____

Love Permits Pain

"We must go through many hardships to enter the kingdom of God." - Acts 14:22

Hardship builds character. The endurance of hardship is the making of a person. Where would our faith be if we didn't experience trials that would test it? Our trials and tribulations develop our faith. The human heart seems to need suffering and brokenness to make it ready to receive God's love and be a blessing to the world. The trials we face reveal where we can grow. God always changes us on the inside before He changes our circumstances on the outside. This process of transformative change begins with trusting Him and trusting that He will take us through everything we face victoriously.

Reflect:

How have hardships shaped you? Have you become a more loving and compassionate person as a result of your trials? How do you know?

Pray:

Heavenly Father, I don't like trials and hardships, but I do know that You are with me in them. I ask for Your strength and perseverance in the midst of life's hardships. In Jesus' name, I pray. Amen.

Declare:

I can do hard things. I am more than a conqueror.

I am thankful for...

_____

_____

_____

_____

_____

Prayer Requests...

_____

_____

_____

_____

_____

What is God's Word saying to you today?...

_____

_____

_____

_____

_____

_____

He Fights for Us

"For the Lord your God is the one who goes with you to fight for you against your enemies to give you victory." - Deuteronomy 20:4

God is greater than whatever we face here in this world, and He fights for us. If you're in the heat of the battle right now and the enemy is attacking you, know that you are not alone. God is the One who fights on our behalf, constantly shielding, protecting, and strengthening us, even when we can't see or feel His presence. He's given us His powerful and true words, so that we'll have the wisdom to stand strong against the enemy. Do not fear the cruel attacks from dark forces. Light defeats darkness every time. Keep shining His light in the face of the enemy and be more than a conqueror in and through Him.

Reflect:

What do you do when you are facing an enemy attack? How do you know when you're under attack?

Pray:

Heavenly Father, I am so grateful that the battle belongs to You. Thank you for covering me during every battle I face. Remind me that the battle is Yours so that I can walk through it with my head held high. In Jesus' name, I pray. Amen.

Declare:

I am not shaken by enemy attacks because I walk with the LORD and am covered in His full armor, knowing the battle belongs to Him.

I am thankful for...

_____

_____

_____

_____

_____

Prayer Requests...

_____

_____

_____

_____

_____

What is God's Word saying to you today?...

_____

_____

_____

_____

_____

_____

Daily Habits for God's Plan

"Your word is a lamp to my feet and a light for my path."
- Psalm 119:105

God wants to bless you with His best. The daily habits you choose will lead you toward or away from His abundant blessings. God wants you to have goals that align with the dream He planted in your heart. He will provide His favor when we do our part to seek and obey Him.

"I press on toward the goal to win the prize for which God has called me." - Philippians 3:14

Set your goals in prayer and work toward them daily with God's help.

Reflect:

What are your daily habits that keep you moving forward in God's plan for your life?

Pray:

Heavenly Father, I know my daily habits are important when it comes to knowing and living in Your will. I ask that You help me develop daily habits that keep my heart burning strong for You, regardless of what is going on around me. In Jesus' name, I pray. Amen.

Declare:

I press on. I persevere. I run my race.

I am thankful for...

_____

_____

_____

_____

_____

Prayer Requests...

_____

_____

_____

_____

_____

What is God's Word saying to you today?...

_____

_____

_____

_____

_____

_____

Live by Faith

"See, the enemy is puffed up; his desires are not upright—but the righteous person will live by his faithfulness." - Habakkuk 2:4

To live our best life, we need to fully trust and obey God. Faith is necessary for this to happen. True faith begins when we are willing to listen and act. Living by faith increases our faith. Our choice to live by faith leads to abundant blessings and favor from God.

Reflect:

What are the benefits of trusting and obeying God? What do you need to do today to take another step of obedience in faith? What has God placed on your heart to do that you may be putting off or resisting?

Pray:

Heavenly Father, I am thankful that You are patient with me. I want to walk in obedient trust with You. I ask that You reveal the next step I need to take to live my best life. I ask You to reveal any areas in my life where I'm not fully trusting and obeying You. Speak to me, Lord, for I am listening. In Jesus' name, I pray. Amen.

Declare:

I always choose faith over fear. I am confident in my choices because I seek God's will and know He is guiding me. I consistently choose His ways, knowing they are higher and better than my own.

I am thankful for...

_____

_____

_____

_____

_____

Prayer Requests...

_____

_____

_____

_____

_____

What is God's Word saying to you today?...

_____

_____

_____

_____

_____

_____

Serve Others

"Then He poured water into the washbasin and began to wash the disciples' feet and to wipe them with the [servant's] towel with which He was girded." - John 13:5

We must serve one another. Serving others is not always viewed as a high position, but Jesus said it is the highest of all. The whole purpose behind serving others is to show them the love that God has shown us. When we are busy washing feet, we have no time to judge and criticize others.

Reflect:

How can you love people more through acts of service?

Pray:

Heavenly Father, thank You for providing opportunities every day for me to serve others in love. I pray that I am present in each moment so that I can see every opportunity that You place on my path to be in service to others for Your namesake. In Jesus' name, I pray. Amen.

Declare:

I am focused, present, and ready to serve others in love each day.

I am thankful for...

_____

_____

_____

_____

_____

Prayer Requests...

_____

_____

_____

_____

_____

What is God's Word saying to you today?...

_____

_____

_____

_____

_____

_____

Love others

"And on her tongue is the law of kindness." - Proverbs 31:26

Early in the morning, may God put on our hearts thoughts of how we can bless others through acts of love. Writing things down that He places on our hearts is a good way to grow in Him and find clarity in the direction that He is guiding us to go. As we ask Him to lead us in the way we should go, our purpose and vision grows clear. Speak life into all that is growing in your heart as a result of Him showing you where you need to go. He will lead you to your highest purpose. He will lead you to love others as He loves you.

Reflect:

How do You want me to love others today?

Pray:

Heavenly Father, I desire to glorify You in the way I live. Help me love others the way that You love me. In Jesus' name, I pray. Amen.

Declare:

I am Christ's image bearer. I love others in the way that He loves me.

I am thankful for...

_____

_____

_____

_____

_____

Prayer Requests...

_____

_____

_____

_____

_____

What is God's Word saying to you today?...

_____

_____

_____

_____

_____

_____

In My Weakness, He Is strong

"In the same way, the Spirit helps us in our weakness. We do not know what we ought to pray for, but the Spirit himself intercedes for us through wordless groans." - Romans 8:26

Let your weaknesses be replaced with His strength. God will fight for you. God wants us to come to Him when we are weak, and He will give us strength. He wants us to take rest and refuge in Him.

Our weakness stirs up His compassion for us. He understands how difficult our journey has been. He wants to bless us abundantly. It is through our weakness that His love gets in and makes us strong. Our faith in Him is the essential ingredient that allows us to look forward to the good things He has for us. Face everything with courage and a good attitude, believing you can do everything through Christ who gives you strength. Listen and obey the Word of the Lord and He will light your way.

"God chose the weak things of the world to shame the strong." - 1 Corinthians 1:27

Reflect:

How has God provided strength when you were weak? How did He help you?

Pray:

Heavenly Father, help me recognize where I'm letting my own pride get in the way. I know my weaknesses serve a greater purpose when I surrender them to You. I desire to walk humbly and honestly with You. In Jesus' name, I pray. Amen.

Declare:

I am strong in the Lord. (Ephesians 6:10)

I am thankful for...

_____

_____

_____

_____

_____

Prayer Requests...

_____

_____

_____

_____

_____

What is God's Word saying to you today?...

_____

_____

_____

_____

_____

_____

Your Breakthrough is Coming

"But thanks be to God, who always leads us as captives in Christ's triumphal procession and uses us to spread the aroma of the knowledge of Him everywhere." - 2 Corinthians 2:1

We often make our own plans, but God interrupts our plans with a path that prepares us for our heart's desires. He knows the end from the beginning and will always direct our steps if we cooperate with Him. His ways are higher than our own. We just need to trust and obey as He takes us down the unknown path to our known future. He has an anointed and appointed time for our breakthrough. We can prove our trust in Him as we wait on Him with a joyful and peaceful presence.

Reflect:

How are you cooperating with God? In what ways have you adjusted your plans to give room for His?

Pray:

Heavenly Father, I am so thankful that You guide and give me wisdom just when I need it. Thank you for loving me the way You do. I am committed to taking the path You have prepared for me, because I know it is the best path I can take. It is the only path that will lead me to Your abundant blessings, breakthrough, and victory. I ask that You help me stay on Your path. In Jesus' name, I pray. Amen.

Declare:

My breakthrough is coming. I always triumph in Christ.

I am thankful for...

_____

_____

_____

_____

_____

Prayer Requests...

_____

_____

_____

_____

_____

What is God's Word saying to you today?...

_____

_____

_____

_____

_____

_____

Choose a Positive Attitude

"And now, dear brothers and sisters, one final thing. Fix your thoughts on what is true, and honorable, and right, and pure, and lovely, and admirable. Think about things that are excellent and worthy of praise." - Philippians 4:8

People who are positive and solution-centered are fun to be around. Their energy is contagious. They get things done and they do things with a joyful spirit. If you keep your mind on what you set out to do in alignment with God's word, you will experience much joy and peace in the process of getting things done. A positive attitude is aligned with God's word, so think on things that are true, honorable, just, lovely, pure, right, admirable, excellent, and worthy of praise.

Reflect:

What are you thinking about most often? Are you intentionally choosing your thoughts? What do you do when your thoughts aren't aligned with God's word?

Pray:

Heavenly Father, help me think on things that are aligned with the truth of Your word. I know there is tremendous power in my thinking. Help me get rid of any thoughts that are not from You. In Jesus' name, I pray. Amen.

Declare:

I choose to have a positive attitude, therefore I choose my thoughts and think on things that are true, honorable, just, lovely, pure, right, admirable, excellent, and worthy of praise.

I am thankful for...

_____

_____

_____

_____

_____

Prayer Requests...

_____

_____

_____

_____

_____

What is God's Word saying to you today?...

_____

_____

_____

_____

_____

_____

Be Impeccable with Your Word

"Do not let any unwholesome talk come out of your mouths, but only what is helpful for building others up according to their needs, that it may benefit those who listen." - Ephesians 4:29

"A gossip betrays a confidence; so avoid anyone who talks too much." - Proverbs 20:19

I keep people who enjoy talking about others at a distance. I am not at all a fan of gossip. I like to ask myself, "What is the purpose of saying, hearing, or sharing this information?" I decided years ago that I was going to be impeccable with my word. I am grateful that scripture addresses this behavior that is so harmful in the lives of people who choose to engage in it.

Reflect:

Are you or people you know engaging in gossip and slander? Do you justify this behavior or are you taking steps to correct it? What and whom are you listening to? What is coming out of your mouth? Are you building people up or tearing them down?

Pray:

Heavenly Father, convict my heart when I let unwholesome talk come out of my mouth or enter my ears. I only want to hear and speak words that edify and build others up. In Jesus' name, I pray. Amen.

Declare:

I am impeccable with my word. I speak words that build myself and others up. I turn away and distance myself from those who engage in gossip and slander.

I am thankful for...

_____

_____

_____

_____

_____

Prayer Requests...

_____

_____

_____

_____

_____

What is God's Word saying to you today?...

_____

_____

_____

_____

_____

_____

God Knows and Cares

"For I am convinced that neither death nor life, neither angels nor demons, neither the present nor the future, nor any powers, neither height nor depth, nor anything else in all creation, will be able to separate us from the love of God that is in Christ Jesus our Lord." - Romans 8:38-39

'For I know the plans I have for you,' declares the Lord, 'plans to prosper you and not to harm you, plans to give you hope and a future.' - Jeremiah 29:11

Focus on the word of God. God's ultimate goal is to get us to a point that no matter what is going on, we remain calm and take rest in Him. The power of the Holy Spirit working on the inside of us will keep us calm, for greater is He that is in us than he that is in the world. (1 John 4:4)

When you follow the lead of the Holy Spirit, He will give you the inner strength to do amazing, inspiring and excellent work that you could never do in your own strength.

"If they obey and serve Him, they will spend their days in prosperity and years in pleasantness and joy." – Job 36:11

Reflect:

How are you following the promptings of the Holy Spirit? How are you in tune with hearing the promptings? If you aren't in touch with the guidance of the Holy Spirit, what are you going to do about it?

Pray:

Heavenly Father, I want to hear the promptings of the Holy Spirit and follow them without questioning or reasoning them away. I need Your guidance every day, and I will do my part to stay connected to You as my source so that I can hear Your voice above the noise of the world. In Jesus' name, I pray. Amen.

Declare:

I am led by the Holy Spirit. I obey and serve God. He knows me intimately and cares about me deeply.

I am thankful for...

_____

_____

_____

_____

_____

Prayer Requests...

_____

_____

_____

_____

_____

What is God's Word saying to you today?...

_____

_____

_____

_____

_____

_____

Speak the Truth in Love

"Instead, speaking the truth in love, we will grow to become in every respect the mature body of Him who is the head, that is, Christ." - Ephesians 4:15

Before you speak, pause and examine your motives. Jesus was in the business of lifting and restoring people. His words were always used to help others. Give more credence to the encouragement of a friend than the discouraging words of critics. Before you speak about someone, examine your motives. Are they pure, honorable, noble, and just? Speaking the truth in love will grow the seeds of truth and love. Act with integrity by speaking the truth in love.

Reflect:

In what ways can you grow in speaking the truth in love?

Pray:

Heavenly Father, thank you for showing me that when I speak the truth in love, things fall into place in ways I could never have imagined. I want to be known as a person who can be counted on to always speak Your truth in love to honor and glorify You. I need Your help to consistently speak the truth in love. In Jesus' name, I pray. Amen.

Declare:

I am courageous and kind as I speak the truth in love.

I am thankful for...

_____

_____

_____

_____

_____

Prayer Requests...

_____

_____

_____

_____

_____

What is God's Word saying to you today?...

_____

_____

_____

_____

_____

Do the Right Thing

"And what does the Lord require of you? To act justly and to love mercy and to walk humbly with your God." - Micah 6:8

I want to do the right thing. There is so much confusion and hurt in our world today. LORD, show me what You want me to do and give me a confident spirit to do what You have called me to. I would rather stand with You alone and be judged by the world, than stand with the world and be judged by You. LORD, place my feet on higher ground where I can walk with You on the path You have prepared for me.

Reflect:

What does the Lord require of you? Are you doing what He has called you to do? What does it mean in your life to do the next right thing?

Pray:

Heavenly Father, let Your will be done in and through me. I ask You to show me what You have called me to do. May Your purpose burn a desire so strong in my heart that I can't ignore Your calling. Help me do the next right thing. In Jesus' name, I pray. Amen.

Declare:

I am here to do what God has called me to do. I choose to live my life His way.

I am thankful for...

_____

_____

_____

_____

_____

Prayer Requests...

_____

_____

_____

_____

_____

What is God's Word saying to you today?...

_____

_____

_____

_____

_____

_____

Walk in the Spirit

"Since we live by the Spirit, let us keep in step with the Spirit."
- Galatians 5:25

To walk in the spirit is to walk away from sin and toward the truth of God's word. Walk towards the light of the world, which is the love of Jesus. Jesus said that He is the light of the world. Walk in prayer and total dependence upon the Lord. Seek Christ in prayer and meditate on God's Word. He responds to those who diligently seek Him. Let God's presence shine from within you onto others today in a way that they can experience a glimpse of His radiant light.

Reflect:

What does walk in the spirit mean to you? How can you turn away from sin and toward the truth of God's word?

Pray:

Heavenly Father, help me turn away from sin and anything that keeps me from walking in the spirit. I want to live my life in Your presence. I want to walk in the spirit with You. In Jesus' name, I pray. Amen.

Declare:

I turn away from sin and toward the truth of God's word. I live in the presence of the Lord.

I am thankful for...

_____

_____

_____

_____

_____

Prayer Requests...

_____

_____

_____

_____

_____

What is God's Word saying to you today?...

_____

_____

_____

_____

_____

_____

Pray and Seek His Face

"If my people, who are called by my name, will humble themselves and pray and seek my face and turn from their wicked ways, then I will hear from heaven, and I will forgive their sin and will heal their land." - 2 Chronicles 7:14

Prayers get answered when they come from an earnest and pure place. Prayers get answered when we pray with belief and unwavering faith in the power of the name of Jesus. Prayers always get answered in His way and in His time. Prayer is powerful. When we begin to see the fruit of our prayers, we will develop a desire to pray unceasingly. Today is a great day to pray in a deeper way.

Reflect:

What is the best way to strengthen your prayer life? Should you start a prayer journal? Do you need to set aside time to pray?

Pray:

Heavenly Father, help me turn away from wicked ways and pray. I want my prayer life to be strengthened. I want to have a prayer life that avails much, because I choose to trust and follow You. In Jesus' name, I pray. Amen.

Declare:

I am a prayer warrior. My prayer life is strong. God hears and answers my prayers.

I am thankful for...

_____

_____

_____

_____

_____

Prayer Requests...

_____

_____

_____

_____

_____

What is God's Word saying to you today?...

_____

_____

_____

_____

_____

_____

Focus on the Good

"Everything good comes from God. Every perfect gift is from him. These good gifts come down from the Father who made all the lights in the sky. But God never changes like the shadows from those lights." - James 1:17

"May the God of hope fill you with all joy and peace as you trust in him, so that you may overflow with hope by the power of the Holy Spirit." - Romans 15:13

What we focus on grows stronger in our lives, so we have a great opportunity to focus on all the good gifts that come from our Father. Every good thing comes from Him. Notice the good and say thank you to God. May His goodness chase you down and overtake you, filling you with a peace that surpasses all understanding, as you place your thoughts on all that is good and praiseworthy.

Reflect:

What happens as you shift your attention to the good things in your life? Why is it important to show gratitude for God's blessings that come your way?

Pray:

Heavenly Father, I know You love me and send so many blessings into my life. I want to show You genuine gratitude for every good thing You send my way. Help me learn to receive Your blessings with grace and humility. In Jesus' name, I pray. Amen.

Declare:

I am worthy of every good thing God has for me. I receive His blessings with grace and gratitude.

I am thankful for...

_____

_____

_____

_____

_____

Prayer Requests...

_____

_____

_____

_____

_____

What is God's Word saying to you today?...

_____

_____

_____

_____

_____

_____

Choose to Be Happy

"Happy are the people whose God is the Lord." - Psalm 144:15

"But all who find safety in you will rejoice; they can always sing for joy. Protect those who love you; because of you they are truly happy." - Psalm 5:11

When we choose to be happy in the Lord, we choose to glorify God, and in turn, we experience His light illuminating from within. The light overtakes any darkness inside of us and begins to radiate outwardly into the world. This is when we are able to let His light shine so that others may see, feel, and be drawn to Him. The deep inner happiness that we desire is a happiness that can be experienced when we are living a Christ-centered life. When we choose to be happy in the Lord, we are choosing happiness that grows and can be shared with others.

Reflect:

When you experience happiness, is it temporary and shallow or is it deep and meaningful? How do you know?

Pray:

Heavenly Father, thank you for abiding in me. Thank you for defeating the darkness within and lighting me up from the inside out. I choose to be happy in You. Help me radiate Your light, like warm sunbeams, onto those You place on my path. In Jesus' name, I pray. Amen.

Declare:

I choose to be happy in the Lord. I have so much light within that it can't help but spill over onto others.

I am thankful for...

_____

_____

_____

_____

_____

Prayer Requests...

_____

_____

_____

_____

_____

What is God's Word saying to you today?...

_____

_____

_____

_____

_____

_____

Learn to Receive

"And God *is* able to make all grace abound toward you, that you, always having all sufficiency in all *things,* may have an abundance for every good work." - 2 Corinthians 9:8

One way we show our love for God is to learn to receive His favor and blessings gracefully. God wants us to receive His grace. When we learn to receive gracefully, we allow God's love to flow through the giver to the receiver, and the blessings God has for each of us is magnified in a beautiful way for both the giver and the receiver. Don't block God's blessings by limiting your giving and receiving. He is a God of abundance, so let His blessings flow.

Reflect:

Are you blocking God's blessings somehow? Why is it important to learn to receive God's blessings with thanksgiving and grace?

Pray:

Heavenly Father, I do not want to get in my own way. I ask You to show me where I may be blocking Your blessings so that I am open and ready to gracefully receive every good thing You shower upon me. In Jesus' name, I pray. Amen.

Declare:

I am worthy of God's grace and favor.

I am thankful for...

_____

_____

_____

_____

_____

Prayer Requests...

_____

_____

_____

_____

_____

What is God's Word saying to you today?...

_____

_____

_____

_____

_____

_____

Arise and Shine

"Arise, shine, for your light has come, and the glory of the Lord rises upon you." - Isaiah 60:1

We have the power to change lives every single day. Let us use our power for good by extending love, grace, mercy, truth, and justice through acts of genuine kindness. Let us be intentional about speaking uplifting words of life to the people we are with throughout the day. Only when we are wide awake can we seize the opportunity to be the light in this dark world. Arise and let the light of Jesus shine in and through you!

Reflect:

In what ways do you experience the glory of the Lord shining upon you? How are you shining His light upon others? If you haven't thought about this much, how can you be more intentional in shining His light?

Pray:

Heavenly Father, thank you for shining upon me. In the same way that You shine upon me, may I shine upon others. Help me receive Your light and love in abundance, until it is overflowing, so that I may shine Your light upon all those You place on my path. In Jesus' name, I pray. Amen.

Declare:

I am filled with the light of Jesus. I shine His light upon all who cross my path.

I am thankful for...

_____

_____

_____

_____

_____

Prayer Requests...

_____

_____

_____

_____

What is God's Word saying to you today?...

_____

_____

_____

_____

_____

_____

A Holy Spirit Makeover

"But the fruit of the Spirit is love, joy, peace, forbearance, kindness, goodness, faithfulness, gentleness, and self-control." - Galatians 5:22

Only the Spirit of God can transform our lives by being born again in the image of Christ. I long to live each day in Christ's image.

Do not worry about what people think. The Holy Spirit makeover takes time and is often hidden at first. Eventually, abundant fruit will blossom if we stay on the path of life in Him, letting His spirit fill us with joy and peace. God has a wonderful plan for us. Each step of faith we take will reveal more of God's beautiful plan. His presence is with us every day and every step of the way as we continue to lean on, walk with, and follow Him.

Reflect:

Have you been born again? Have you felt the presence of the Holy Spirit abiding in you? Do you long for a Holy Spirit makeover? Why or why not?

Pray:

Heavenly Father, I know You have begun a good work in me. I'm grateful You will never leave me and that You will continue this Holy Spirit makeover throughout my life here on earth. I want to be made more and more into Your image as I live life. I need Your help every step of the way. In Jesus' name, I pray. Amen.

Declare:

I am glowing with the Holy Spirit. When people see me, they see Him.

I am thankful for...

_____

_____

_____

_____

_____

Prayer Requests...

_____

_____

_____

_____

_____

What is God's Word saying to you today?...

_____

_____

_____

_____

_____

_____

Path to Prosperity

"Keep this Book of the Law always on your lips; meditate on it day and night, so that you may be careful to do everything written in it. Then you will be prosperous and successful."
– Joshua 1:8

If we put God first, prosperity will follow. The Bible has everything we need to live a prosperous and successful life. It is our job as Christians to meditate on the word of God, day and night. If we meditate on His word, and live by it, we are choosing a prosperous and successful path. With God as our source, we are moving in step with Him and will experience all that He has prepared for us.

Reflect:

What does it mean to keep the Book of the Law always on your lips? How do you meditate on His word day and night? What does it mean to you to live a prosperous and successful life?

Pray:

Heavenly Father, I am so thankful for Your word and the promises that are provided by You in Your word. I want my life to be ordered by You. In Jesus' name, I pray. Amen.

Declare:

I am prosperous and successful.

I am thankful for...

_____

_____

_____

_____

_____

Prayer Requests...

_____

_____

_____

_____

_____

What is God's Word saying to you today?...

_____

_____

_____

_____

_____

_____

God Has Planted You

"Each person should remain in the situation they were in when God called them." – 1 Corinthians 7:20

God has you where you are today on purpose. He wants you to be His light. He has uniquely equipped you to fulfill your assignment. Loving like He does is as simple as taking time to invest in people's everyday lives. When you encounter people throughout the day, always be listening for the Spirit's prompting, and you'll see more and more opportunities to be His light.

Reflect:

How do I know that God has planted me in the place I am in today in life? What can I do to make the most of this season?

Pray:

Heavenly Father, I place my trust in You alone, for I know You have placed me where I am in life today. I will make the most of this season in my life by listening to Your Holy Spirit promptings as I go about my day. Help me live my life for You. In Jesus' name, I pray. Amen.

Declare:

I live my life to honor and glorify His name. I do good work where I am planted.

I am thankful for...

_____

_____

_____

_____

_____

Prayer Requests...

_____

_____

_____

_____

_____

What is God's Word saying to you today?...

_____

_____

_____

_____

_____

_____

The Steps of Faith

"Now faith is confidence in what we hope for and assurance about what we do not see." - Hebrew 11:1

Steps of faith lead to the unknown. They can lead us into what appears to be, darkness and disaster, but God will reveal the path and will work everything together for our good when we put our trust in Him.

Let us move in faith today, not knowing or seeing, but trusting.

Reflect:

How are you taking steps of faith? What do you hope for? Do you trust the path you are on? What is one step of faith God is urging you to take? How do you know? What's stopping you from taking it?

Pray:

Heavenly Father, help me take steps of faith even when it seems that my faith is only the size of a mustard seed. I know it says in Your word that faith the size of a mustard seed is enough faith to move mountains. Help me move the mountains in front of me with my faith that feels so small at times. In Jesus' name, I pray. Amen.

Declare:

I am confident that I am taking steps of faith that are ordered by God and are leading to my destiny.

I am thankful for...

_____

_____

_____

_____

_____

Prayer Requests...

_____

_____

_____

_____

_____

What is God's Word saying to you today?...

_____

_____

_____

_____

_____

_____

Call Out to Jesus

"Everyone who calls on the name of the Lord will be saved."
- Romans 10:13

When we call out to Jesus, He will refresh us, heal us, and strengthen us. He will give us peace and joy. He will get us back on the path to fulfilling our purpose. He will make what is hard, easy. He calms the storm. He makes possible, what we consider impossible. Call out to the Lord and be saved.

Reflect:

When have you called out to the Lord? What happened when you did? If you haven't, why not?

Pray:

Heavenly Father, thank you for being there for me every time I call out to You. I love You and need You every day of my life. Help me call out to You instead of trying to do things in my own strength. In Jesus' name, I pray. Amen.

Declare:

Jesus has saved and set me free.

I am thankful for...

_____

_____

_____

_____

_____

Prayer Requests...

_____

_____

_____

_____

_____

What is God's Word saying to you today?...

_____

_____

_____

_____

_____

_____

Let God Heal Your Heart

"I will give them an undivided heart and put a new spirit in them; I will remove from them their heart of stone and give them a heart of flesh." - Ezekiel 11:19

When we seek God and allow Him to heal our heart from past pain and sin, we will grow in faith, hope, health, and love. As we give ourselves over to Him each day, He will take up greater space in us. When this happens, our lives begin to change, as we are being transformed into His image. Those around us will see the changes as we shine the light of His presence in our everyday interaction with others. As we heal, others begin to heal around us. God's love will flow through us in a supernatural way as we live loved and lifted in Him.

Reflect:

Do you have a heart that needs to be healed? Are you willing to let God in to begin the healing process? What does your heart desire?

Pray:

Heavenly Father, You know my heart. Thank you for beginning a good work in me. The layers of healing are so complex and deep. Please continue to purify my heart. I want to grow stronger and more whole, in You, throughout life. In Jesus' name, I pray. Amen.

Declare:

I have the Spirit of God living in me. My heart is strong, healthy, and whole.

I am thankful for...

_____

_____

_____

_____

_____

Prayer Requests...

_____

_____

_____

_____

What is God's Word saying to you today?...

_____

_____

_____

_____

_____

_____

Purify My Heart

"Blessed are the pure in heart, for they shall see God." - Matthew 5:8

Our heart, our innermost being, is the root of all our actions. For our motives to be pure, our heart must be pure. God wants to give us a pure heart. He wants to restore, redeem, and purify our hearts and minds. As we repent and submit to Him, He begins a great work within us day by day.

What we see, hear, and meditate on matters. Who we spend time with and seek counsel from matters. Guard your heart above all else. (Proverbs 4:23)

Reflect:

How's your heart? What are you feeding it?

Pray:

Heavenly Father, thank you for beginning a good work in my heart. May the fire You ignited in my heart always burn passionately for everything that represents You. In Jesus' name, I pray. Amen.

Declare:

I have a pure heart that represents Christ.

I am thankful for...

_____

_____

_____

_____

_____

Prayer Requests...

_____

_____

_____

_____

_____

What is God's Word saying to you today?...

_____

_____

_____

_____

_____

_____

Reflect His Image

"So God created mankind in his own image, in the image of God he created them; male and female he created them." - Genesis 1:27

Be determined to let God work through you. God sees us according to our hearts. He knows us deeply and intimately. If we have faith in Him and surrender to His will, He will work wonders through us.

Be a person who treats others with dignity and stands up for what is right in life. Be a person whose convictions are based on God's Word and do what God calls you to do.

Reflect:

How are you reflecting His image?

Pray:

Heavenly Father, I want to be Your image bearer. Help me learn Your ways so that I can know how to represent You well. In Jesus' name, I pray. Amen.

Declare:

I am Christ's image bearer.

I am thankful for...

_____

_____

_____

_____

_____

Prayer Requests...

_____

_____

_____

_____

_____

What is God's Word saying to you today?...

_____

_____

_____

_____

_____

_____

God Meets Us in Our Sorrow

"He heals the brokenhearted and binds up their wounds."
- Psalm 147:3

"The Lord is near to the brokenhearted and saves those who are crushed in spirit." - Psalm 34:18

God longs to give us joy, to meet us in our sorrow, and give us the power of His Holy Spirit. He walks us through the valley of devastation, destruction, and darkness into His glorious light. He wants to take us through to the other side, where joy, peace, love, and hope abound. He promises us healing, wholeness, and victory.

Reflect:

Are you willing to turn to God and let Him meet you in your sorrow?

Pray:

Heavenly Father, I come before You today in need of Your healing hand. In You, all things are possible. Hold my heart within Yours, and renew my mind, body, and spirit. Give me the strength to move forward on the path You've laid out for me. Guide my steps and give me the wisdom to identify those You've placed around me to help me live my best life. In Jesus' name, I pray. Amen.

Declare:

I am healed and whole.

I am thankful for...

_____

_____

_____

_____

_____

Prayer Requests...

_____

_____

_____

_____

_____

What is God's Word saying to you today?...

_____

_____

_____

_____

_____

_____

Delight in the Lord

"Take delight in the Lord, and He will give you the desires of your heart." - Psalm 37:4

We will receive the desires of our heart when we stay centered and fixed on Him. Taking delight in the Lord means that our hearts truly find fulfillment and peace in Him. Focus on His love and limit distractions that come your way. Resist the need to please others. Pleasing Him is where our attention should be. Genuinely take delight in Him, and He will fulfill the desires of your heart.

Reflect:

How do you take delight in the Lord?

Pray:

Heavenly Father, I desire to please You. When I become distracted, please help me pause and focus my attention back on You. I know that You are the way to the lasting fulfillment and joy that my heart desires. May I remain centered in Your everlasting love. In Jesus' name, I pray. Amen.

Declare:

I have all of my needs met by God. I delight in the Lord.

I am thankful for...

_____

_____

_____

_____

_____

Prayer Requests...

_____

_____

_____

_____

What is God's Word saying to you today?...

_____

_____

_____

_____

_____

_____

Taken Aside by Jesus

"He took him aside, away from the crowd." - Mark 7:33

God took me aside and began a good work in my heart. It was in my alone time of solitude with Him that I began to read, write, and pray. It was in this alone time with God that I was able to a get to a deeper understanding of who He really is. God has rekindled the flames within my heart in this place of solitude. It was painful at first. I did not like being alone to face the truth within myself. I tried to run from it. Thankfully, He held me close and I didn't get far when I did run. His course corrections came quickly and swiftly. A few years later, I now seek alone time with Him. Instead of running away, I run toward Him into the peace that this time alone with Him provides.

Reflect:

Do you have alone time with God? Why or why not?

Pray:

Heavenly Father, thank you for loving me the way You do. I used to fear being alone. I now realize I need alone time with You daily. I need You to continue to take me aside so that I can remain centered in Your divine purpose. In Jesus' name, I pray. Amen.

Declare:

I am never alone. He is always with me.

I am thankful for...

_____

_____

_____

_____

_____

Prayer Requests...

_____

_____

_____

_____

_____

What is God's Word saying to you today?...

_____

_____

_____

_____

_____

_____

Live out the Love of God

"The love of God has been poured out in our hearts by the Holy Spirit who was given to us." - Romans 5:5

Show others the power of the Holy Spirit to transform lives. Share your testimony. Live with such radical faith that the power of God is evident to all.

Live out the love of God through:
- the conversations you have
- the acts of kindness you show
- the prayers you pray
- the forgiveness you extend
- the generosity you give
- the way you walk
- the way you love
- the way you serve
- the way you live

Your faith lived actively will demonstrate that God is flowing through your heart.

If we love God, we should be loving people. If we get involved in genuinely loving people, we can influence the world to be transformed for the glory of God.

Reflect:

How are you genuinely loving people?

Pray:

Heavenly Father, I thank You for pouring Your love into me in such a powerful way that the Holy Spirit works through me to demonstrate Your love for people. Help me walk in the Spirit with absolute integrity, so that through the way I live, others may come to know You. In Jesus' name, I pray. Amen.

Declare:

I have a fierce faith that burns bright as I live out the love of God.

I am thankful for...

_____

_____

_____

_____

_____

Prayer Requests...

_____

_____

_____

_____

_____

What is God's Word saying to you today?...

_____

_____

_____

_____

_____

_____

Take Me into the Deep

"They that go down to the sea in ships, that do business in great waters; these see the works of the Lord, and his wonders in the deep." - Psalm 107:23-24

Every wind that blows is guiding us towards our destination. We have an amazing destiny when we follow God's plan for our life. We must believe in Him in the midst of the storm. The trials we go through grow and prepare us for where God is taking us. Trust Him and pass the challenging test by remaining Christlike in the midst of persecution. Our faith is tested greatly in the midst of our trials. Fear will keep us in the shallow, while faith will take us into the deep.

Reflect:

Are you staying near the shore or are you going into the deep? How do you know? Can you see the shore? Are you still living in shallow waters?

Pray:

Heavenly Father, send me into the deep where there is plenty of room to win a glorious victory for Your namesake. I know that it will be stormy and scary at times, but I want to go where You are, where my trust is without borders. In Jesus' name, I pray. Amen.

Declare:

I am determined to go into the deep with the Lord.

I am thankful for...

_____

_____

_____

_____

_____

Prayer Requests...

_____

_____

_____

_____

_____

What is God's Word saying to you today?...

_____

_____

_____

_____

_____

_____

Ask God for Big Things

"Now to him who is able to do immeasurably more than all we ask or imagine, according to his power that is at work within us." - Ephesians 3:20

Dream big and then even bigger. We need to think big, ask for big, and hope for even bigger. We then need to pray, wait, and work hard for what we desire. Sometimes, we don't ask God for big things because we don't feel like we deserve them. That is something that we all deal with from time to time, but it is a feeling and it is not how God intended it to be for us. He wants us to put our faith in His promises. It's important to turn to God for the healing that we need to feel worthy of asking him for big things.

Reflect:

Why is it important to ask God for big things? What do big things represent in your life?

Pray:

Heavenly Father, right now I don't feel like I deserve big things from You. I know that my feelings don't indicate the truth of what You have planned for me. I trust You to do the big things in my life that only You can do. I ask that You prepare my heart to receive every good thing You have for me and to feel worthy of Your unconditional love. In Jesus' name, I pray. Amen.

Declare:

I am worthy of big things. God loves me unconditionally.

I am thankful for...

_____

_____

_____

_____

_____

Prayer Requests...

_____

_____

_____

_____

_____

What is God's Word saying to you today?...

_____

_____

_____

_____

_____

_____

Start Your Day with God

"Be very careful, then, how you live—not as unwise but as wise, making the most of every opportunity, because the days are evil." - Ephesians 5:15-16

Starting your day with God will keep you centered in Him throughout the day. You will be more likely to walk with wisdom and discernment in the Holy Spirit, making the most of how you spend your time. Time will be maximized in living your authentic purpose when you start your day with God.

Reflect:

Why is it important to start your day with God?

Pray:

Heavenly Father, I need You. I know how important it is to start my day with You, regardless of how I feel. It's especially important during the times when I'm struggling that I immediately put my complete faith and trust in Your promises. Help me, Lord, to seek Your face no matter how I feel. Help me continue to choose to begin my day with You. In Jesus' name, I pray. Amen.

Declare:

I am filled with God's wisdom.

I am thankful for...

_____

_____

_____

_____

_____

Prayer Requests...

_____

_____

_____

_____

_____

What is God's Word saying to you today?...

_____

_____

_____

_____

_____

Start with the Truth

"And you will know the Truth, and the Truth will set you free."
- John 8.32

Change begins with the truth. We must face the truth about who we are. In the process of making changes for the better, the hardest part is often facing the truth about ourselves. We don't need to be ashamed about who we are. We simply need to own our truth and begin to work through it by repenting and asking for God's forgiveness...and then we need to get excited about change.

When we take responsibility for our choices that led to where we are, we can face the truth and be set free. Ask God to reveal the truth about you. We often seek the truth about others while ignoring ourselves, when we really need to start with ourselves. We may feel a great deal of pain as He reveals the truth about who we are, but this pain is a healing pain that will lead to peace and joy if we stay committed to doing the hard, yet necessary, work.

Reflect:

What is the truth that you need to face today?

Pray:

Heavenly Father, help me see and admit the truth about myself in all areas of my life. I am committed to seeking and trusting You to lead me through the changes I need to make to prosper my heart and soul in You. In Jesus' name, I pray. Amen.

Declare:

I am aligned with God's truth. I seek, speak and live His truth.

I am thankful for...

_____

_____

_____

_____

_____

Prayer Requests...

_____

_____

_____

_____

_____

What is God's Word saying to you today?...

_____

_____

_____

_____

_____

_____

Lean on Him

"Lean on, trust in, and be confident in the Lord with all your heart and mind and do not rely on your own insight or understanding." - Proverbs 3:5

I need to lean on the Lord. There are many times when I'm not sure what to do. For me, what has worked is to read scripture, and listen to messages and music that point me to His love. Prayer, in the form of conversation, with God also helps me lean on Him. When I pray, I tend to do most of the talking. I think that is because listening to Him is a unique form of communication that I'm learning to understand the more time I spend with Him. His answers don't always come immediately and rarely come in the way I expect them to. One thing I am learning, firsthand, is that He hears me and always answers in His way and in His time.

Reflect:

How do you lean on the Lord?

Pray:

Heavenly Father, I am so grateful that You are with me at all times. May I learn to lean on You immediately when trouble comes my way. I want to lean on You more and more, knowing that I am stronger when I do so. Help me get out of my own way so that I can consistently lean on and trust in You. In Jesus' name, I pray. Amen.

Declare:

I am confident in the Lord. I lean on and trust in Him.

I am thankful for...

_____

_____

_____

_____

_____

Prayer Requests...

_____

_____

_____

_____

_____

What is God's Word saying to you today?...

_____

_____

_____

_____

_____

_____

You Are Chosen

"Greater is He who is in you than he who is in the world."
- 1 John 4:4

God has chosen you for a Kingdom purpose and nothing can disqualify you from it.

God has a purpose for each one of us. He chose you. He called you by name. He will qualify and empower you to do what He has called you to do with excellence. With God working in you, you have no limitations. Take the limits off of God and do what He leads you to do each day. Living in total dependence on Him is a glorious adventure. When you depend on God continually, your whole perspective changes. You see Him working all around you. You begin each day with excitement and anticipation, waiting to see what He will do. You accept weaknesses as a gift from Him, knowing His power plugs into those weak places and gives a strength that far surpasses anything humanly possible. Choose to consciously live and move in Him, enjoying the intimate adventure He offers.

Reflect:

What has God called you to do? Do you feel like one of His chosen people? Why or why not?

Pray:

Heavenly Father, I am so grateful to now know that You live on the inside of me. I need You to work through me to face each new day. I will begin my day with You and do my best to walk in surrender to You throughout the day. I don't want to limit what You can do in and through me. I need You to do what only You can do. In Jesus' name, I pray. Amen.

Declare:

I am chosen. Jesus lives in me.

I am thankful for...

_____

_____

_____

_____

_____

Prayer Requests...

_____

_____

_____

_____

_____

What is God's Word saying to you today?...

_____

_____

_____

_____

_____

_____

Speak the Word

"Truly I tell you, if anyone says to this mountain, 'Go, throw yourself into the sea,' and does not doubt in their heart but believes that what they say will happen, it will be done for them." - Mark 11:23

Whatever you ask for in prayer, through faith in Jesus' name, you will receive it. You must get in the habit of speaking the Word out loud. Speak it into existence in your life. Take authority by speaking the truth of God's word over your life. We need to take the limits off of God and what we think is possible. With Him, all things are possible for the one who believes. Stand on His promises and declare His Word. He will bring it to pass in His way and in His time.

Reflect:

Do you know the Word? Do you know it well enough to speak it over your life? What can you do to grow in this area?

Pray:

Heavenly Father, thank you for the promises You provide in Your Word. Help me know Your word, meditate on it, and have it living on the inside of me so that I can speak it over my life effortlessly. In Jesus' name, I pray. Amen.

Declare:

I am who God says I am. I believe in the truth of His word.

I am thankful for...

_____

_____

_____

_____

_____

Prayer Requests...

_____

_____

_____

_____

What is God's Word saying to you today?...

_____

_____

_____

_____

_____

Wait in Gratitude

"Blessed are all who wait on him!" - Isaiah 30:18

What God is preparing you for is worth the wait. Exercise faith by putting your confidence and trust in Him. He always works in our lives with our absolute best interests in mind. He is working in your life to bring you the greatest possible blessing. Wait expectantly and with excitement in total gratitude and complete faith for His abundant blessings! While you're waiting, be an example of His love and light in this world, in everyday moments where you have the opportunity to share His love and truth with others.

Reflect:

How are you waiting on the Lord? What are you doing while you wait on the Lord?

Pray:

Heavenly Father, while I wait on You, I choose to wait in total gratitude, knowing that You are working everything together for the good of those who love You. I love You, and while I wait, I will do my best to be an expression of Your truth and love in the lives of all that cross my path. In Jesus' name, I pray. Amen.

Declare:

I am blessed and patient as I wait on the Lord in total gratitude. I am honored to do His work while I wait.

I am thankful for...

_____

_____

_____

_____

_____

Prayer Requests...

_____

_____

_____

_____

What is God's Word saying to you today?...

_____

_____

_____

_____

_____

The Anointing Lives in You

"The anointing which you have received from Him abides in you." - 1 John 2:27

You can see the glow of the anointing and feel His presence abiding in people who are carriers of God's spirit. When His spirit is in us, it affects every area of our lives. When the anointing is in you, it is transferred to others through words and actions that take root in others long after you're gone, because your presence was the living and loving presence of Jesus. Start your day by asking God to give you a fresh anointing, then go out and do the work in the lives of others that He leads you to do.

Reflect:

How are you shining His light? What can you do to be sure that His presence is what you represent?

Pray:

Heavenly Father, I am so grateful to now know that You live on the inside of me. Help me represent You by shining Your light into the lives of the people that You place on my path. Help me be the best representative of You possible. In Jesus' name, I pray. Amen.

Declare:

I am anointed to represent Christ.

I am thankful for...

_____

_____

_____

_____

_____

Prayer Requests...

_____

_____

_____

_____

_____

What is God's Word saying to you today?...

_____

_____

_____

_____

_____

Go the Extra Mile

"Then this Daniel became distinguished above all the other presidents and satraps, because an excellent spirit was in him. And the king planned to set him over the whole kingdom."
- Daniel 6:3

God has called us to live a big life. He is able to do far more than anything we can ask or imagine. We need to live big lives of faith in order to live a life without limits. Choose to go beyond the minimum so you can have a maximum impact for God's kingdom. The extraordinary life happens when we give the extra in all we say and do. There is no room for complacency or mediocrity when living the excellent life God has called us to live.

Reflect:

In what ways are you going the extra mile to live a life of absolute excellence? How can you go the extra mile in your life today? What does going the extra mile mean to you?

Pray:

Heavenly Father, I want to have an excellent spirit like Daniel. Show me where I can go the extra mile in my life, so that I can live the life You have called me to live. In Jesus' name, I pray. Amen.

Declare:

I have a spirit of excellence. I go the extra mile.

I am thankful for...

_____

_____

_____

_____

_____

Prayer Requests...

_____

_____

_____

_____

_____

What is God's Word saying to you today?...

_____

_____

_____

_____

_____

Integrity Matters

"Whoever walks in integrity walks securely, but he who makes his ways crooked will be found out." - Proverbs 10:9

We need to live what we speak. Our actions on every level need to match our hearts on the deepest level. God will bless us if we are people of integrity. We honor God when we live with integrity. A person of integrity is a "whole" person who does not have divided loyalties. People with integrity have nothing to hide and nothing to fear. We are a person of integrity when we live consistently, regardless of the noise. Being a person of integrity in Christ means that we live whole and centered in Him regardless of what comes our way.

Reflect:

Why is it important to be a person of integrity? Is there an area in your life where your actions don't match your heart? How can you align your words and actions more consistently?

Pray:

Heavenly Father, I want to be a person of integrity. I want my heart to match what I say and do. Help me identify areas where I am lacking in integrity. I want to be a person of integrity in every area of my life. I need Your help, Lord, to live with excellence. In Jesus' name, I pray. Amen.

Declare:

I am a person of integrity. I live with excellence in word and deed.

I am thankful for...

_____

_____

_____

_____

_____

Prayer Requests...

_____

_____

_____

_____

_____

What is God's Word saying to you today?...

_____

_____

_____

_____

_____

_____

Slow Down

"You will keep in perfect peace, whose mind is stayed on you." - Isaiah 26:3

Jesus was not in a hurry. He was present with the people in front of Him. Jesus stopped to do the work He was called to do. He knew His purpose. Jesus wasn't in a hurry and He wasn't distracted by the noise. We need to slow down to be more like Jesus. When we rush, we miss out on blessing people and being blessed by them. In order to be the positive change we wish to see in the world, we need to slow down and choose to be a blessing in the lives of those we are near. God puts us on this path and it's our choice to slow down to experience the beauty in it.

Reflect:

Are you in a hurry? How can you slow down and be more present with people?

Pray:

Heavenly Father, help me slow down so I can truly see the beauty that You've placed on my path, and be a blessing to the people I encounter along the way. As I slow down, may I become more like You. In Jesus' name, I pray. Amen.

Declare:

I am at peace and I am present as I slow down and fix my mind on Him.

I am thankful for...

_____

_____

_____

_____

_____

Prayer Requests...

_____

_____

_____

_____

What is God's Word saying to you today?...

_____

_____

_____

_____

_____

_____

Live Victoriously

"For everyone born of God overcomes the world. This is the victory that has overcome the world, even our faith." - 1 John 5:4

We were not created to live defeated, unsatisfactory lives. We were created to have victory over sin, self, and Satan. Victory is not gained by human effort. It is impossible to live this life in our own strength. We need to humble ourselves and realize that God is our strength. It is through Him that we are able to live victoriously. Victory is a gift, it is a choice, and it is gained by fixing our eyes on Jesus.

Reflect:

Are you living victoriously? Why or why not?

Pray:

Heavenly Father, thank you for fighting my battles for me. As I fix my eyes on You, I know that You are victorious in all things that come against me. Thank you for Your word that says no weapon formed against me shall prosper. I place my trust and faith completely in You. In Jesus' name, I pray. Amen.

Declare:

I am victorious.

I am thankful for...

_____

_____

_____

_____

_____

Prayer Requests...

_____

_____

_____

_____

_____

What is God's Word saying to you today?...

_____

_____

_____

_____

_____

His Deepest Truths

"Create in me a pure heart, O God, and renew a steadfast spirit within me." - Psalm 51:10

The fruitful seed falls on good soil, takes deep root, and grows in good and honest hearts. We need to be careful to maintain the soil of our hearts. Those with profound character will be deepened by life's storms. Once God has deepened us, He will give us His deepest truths, and will trust us with greater power to do His work. He will lead us into new depths in our lives and save us from a shallow existence.

Reflect:

How's your heart? Are you living a shallow existence or are you doing the necessary work for a deeper, more meaningful life?

Pray:

Heavenly Father, thank you for abiding in me and giving me a deeper, more meaningful life in You. Thank you for taking me out of the shallow and into the deep with You. Help me to stay with You regardless of the storms that come my way, I do not want to retreat to the comfort that resides in the shallow. In Jesus' name, I pray. Amen.

Declare:

I am in deep with Christ. He has purified my heart.

I am thankful for...

_____

_____

_____

_____

_____

Prayer Requests...

_____

_____

_____

_____

_____

What is God's Word saying to you today?...

_____

_____

_____

_____

_____

_____

His Purpose

"The Lord will fulfill His purpose for me." -Psalm 138:8

It is in the midst of our deep pain that we often find our highest purpose. That is when the Holy Spirit works deep within our soul. This is when our entire being lies perfectly still under the hand of God. This is when He begins a good work in us, a work only He can do to make us whole in Him. He causes everything, good and bad, to work together for our good.

Reflect:

Do you trust that the Lord will fulfill His purpose in you? Have you experienced a time of deep pain in your life where the Lord made His purpose clear to you?

Pray:

Heavenly Father, thank you for beginning a good work in me. I want to continue to go deeper with You so that I may live my life according to Your highest purpose. In Jesus' name, I pray. Amen.

Declare:

I choose God's purpose for my life.

I am thankful for...

_____

_____

_____

_____

_____

Prayer Requests...

_____

_____

_____

_____

_____

What is God's Word saying to you today?...

_____

_____

_____

_____

_____

Unleash Your Gift

"Having then gifts differing according to the grace that is given to us, whether prophecy, [let us prophesy] according to the proportion of faith." - Romans 12:6

By design, God placed gifts inside of us that only we carry. We need to share our gifts. We must never shrink back for the comfort of others. We need what God placed inside of us to be shared with the world. As we share our spiritual gifts, let His love be your highest goal.

"Pursue love, and earnestly desire the spiritual gifts, especially that you may prophesy." - 1 Corinthians 14:1

Reflect:

Are you sharing the gift God gave you with others? What is interfering with you sharing your gift with others?

Pray:

Heavenly Father, I believe You when You say no weapon formed against me will prosper. Help me stay in faith so that I can share my gift completely with others, especially the ones who are difficult to share it with. When they see me, let them see You. In Jesus' name, I pray. Amen.

Declare:

I am anointed with spiritual gifts to represent Christ.

I am thankful for...

_____

_____

_____

_____

_____

Prayer Requests...

_____

_____

_____

_____

_____

What is God's Word saying to you today?...

_____

_____

_____

_____

_____

_____

Trust in Him

"Trust in the Lord with all your heart and lean not on your own understanding; in all your ways acknowledge Him, and He will make your paths straight." - Proverbs 3:5-6

Trust in Him with all your heart and He will make your path straight. What matters most is doing what God says, knowing He is faithful to do what He has promised. This is one of my favorite verses. I find myself at times of uncertainty saying this verse out loud. I'm grateful for the opportunities that I can trust in His ways being higher than my own.

Reflect:

Are you trusting in the Lord with all your heart? How are you acknowledging Him in all your ways? Do you trust in Him to make your path straight, especially when your path appears to be uncertain?

Pray:

Heavenly Father, I trust You to make my path straight. I trust You with all my heart and lean not on my own understanding. Help me to acknowledge and seek You in all ways throughout the day. May I never be too busy to be in Your presence. In Jesus' name, I pray. Amen.

Declare:

I trust in the Lord with all my heart.

I am thankful for...

_____

_____

_____

_____

_____

Prayer Requests...

_____

_____

_____

_____

What is God's Word saying to you today?...

_____

_____

_____

_____

_____

In the Darkness

"I will never leave you nor forsake you." - Hebrews 13:5

By faith, we know He's there. Whether or not we feel His presence, we know He is there and that He is working on our behalf. Hold on. Trust. Reach out to Him. Believe the truth of God's Word over the facts of your circumstances or the logic of what your mind may be trying to tell you. Choose God's word over reasoning, fear and doubt.

Reflect:

Do you believe He will never leave you or forsake you? How can you build healthy habits by turning to Him when things are dark in your life?

Pray:

Heavenly Father, I know You are there for me, even when I can't see You, even when I can't feel You, I know You are with me. When things appear dark, I want to feel Your light burning from within. I will trust You, knowing that You will never leave me nor forsake me. In Jesus' name, I pray. Amen.

Declare:

I know God is always with me.

I am thankful for...

_____

_____

_____

_____

_____

Prayer Requests...

_____

_____

_____

_____

_____

What is God's Word saying to you today?...

_____

_____

_____

_____

_____

_____

Shine Bright

"The path of the righteous is like the morning sun, shining ever brighter till the full light of day. But the way of the wicked is like deep darkness; they do not know what makes them stumble." - Proverbs 4:18-19

Don't worry about the wicked. They don't even know what makes them stumble. Keep walking in the truth of God's ways. The path of the righteous is the path that defeats darkness. Keep smiling and keep shining in the midst of enemy attacks. Seek His face and you will not stumble. You don't even need to know what the enemy is up to. Trust that God knows and He is your protector. He will not allow any weapon formed against you to prosper, so let Him fight for you while you continue to shine bright.

Reflect:

What does shine bright mean to you? Have you allowed any darkness to dim your light?

Pray:

Heavenly Father, I want to shine Your light into this world. I don't want to spend any of my time trying to play the games that the enemy plays. I am grateful that I can put my faith in You to fight the battles that come my way. I live for You. Help me stay focused on Your love and truth so that I can always walk in Your ways. In Jesus' name, I pray. Amen.

Declare:

I shine bright in the presence of the enemy. Darkness trembles when I am near.

I am thankful for...

_____

_____

_____

_____

_____

Prayer Requests...

_____

_____

_____

_____

_____

What is God's Word saying to you today?...

_____

_____

_____

_____

_____

_____

In the Morning

"And be ready in the morning, and come up in the morning unto mount Sinai, and present thyself there to me in the top of the mount." - Exodus 34:2

God renews our strength each morning. He wants us to start our day with Him so He can give us a new supply of energy. Blessed is the day when the morning is set apart for God. Successful is the day when the first victory is given by starting our day in prayer.

Reflect:

How are you starting your day? Do you need to do anything differently?

Pray:

Heavenly Father, I know how important it is to start my day with You. No matter what I do, or how much time I spend, help me stay focused on starting my day with You. May I always know that You are my source and that I need to be filled with Your strength before I begin each day. In Jesus' name, I pray. Amen.

Declare:

I seek God first.

I am thankful for...

_____

_____

_____

_____

_____

Prayer Requests...

_____

_____

_____

_____

What is God's Word saying to you today?...

_____

_____

_____

_____

_____

_____

Be Positive

"Keep your heart with all vigilance, for from it flow the springs of life." - Proverbs 4:23

Being positive doesn't mean you are happy all the time. Being positive is a choice, knowing that better days are coming. When we choose to protect our heart and mind by focusing on all that is good, lovely, and pure, we are able to stay connected to His spirit. His joyful spirit abides in us. He makes being positive effortless, even in the midst of challenging circumstances.

"A joyful heart is good medicine, but a crushed spirit dries up the bones." - Proverbs 17:22

Reflect:

Are you paying attention to what you're paying attention to? How can you choose to be more positive each day?

Pray:

Heavenly Father, I want my positivity to be authentic. I choose to be positive to honor You. I want to glorify and magnify Your presence in my life and in the lives of those around me. Thank you for abiding in me with Your joyful, loving, and positive spirit. Help me to stay focused on You as my source. In Jesus' name, I pray. Amen.

Declare:

I am positive and filled with joy.

I am thankful for...

_____

_____

_____

_____

_____

Prayer Requests...

_____

_____

_____

_____

_____

What is God's Word saying to you today?...

_____

_____

_____

_____

_____

_____

Be You

You were created in His image.

"So God created man in his own image, in the image of God he created him; male and female he created them." - Genesis 1:27

You are fearfully and wonderfully made.

"For you formed my inward parts; you knitted me together in my mother's womb. I praise you, for I am fearfully and wonderfully made. Wonderful are your works; my soul knows it very well. My frame was not hidden from you, when I was being made in secret, intricately woven in the depths of the earth. Your eyes saw my unformed substance; in your book were written, every one of them, the days that were formed for me, when as yet there was none of them." - Psalm 139:13-16

- You matter
- You are a treasure
- You are loved
- You are valuable
- You make a difference
- You are a warrior
- You are fearless
- You are a blessing
- You are strong
- You are amazing
- You are never alone
- You are chosen

- You are redeemed
- You are favored
- You are blessed
- You are healed
- You were designed with a purpose
- You are fearfully and wonderfully made

He created you.
He calls you.
He equips you.
He empowers you.
He rewards you.
He strengthens you.

Reflect:

Do you realize how much you truly matter? Are you living to your full potential? What can you do to move closer to who He created you to be?

Pray:

Heavenly Father, I know You designed me with a purpose and that purpose is to glorify You. Help me see all of the wonderful things about me that make me unique and one-of-a-kind to do what only I can do in this world to lead others to You. In Jesus' name, I pray. Amen.

Declare:

I am fearfully and wonderfully made in His image.

I am thankful for...

_____

_____

_____

_____

_____

Prayer Requests...

_____

_____

_____

_____

_____

What is God's Word saying to you today?...

_____

_____

_____

_____

_____

_____

Let God Fill Your Heart

"There is no fear in love. But perfect love drives out fear, because fear has to do with punishment. The one who fears is not made perfect in love." - 1 John 4:18

When God's love fills your heart, it takes up every part of it with the presence of His Holy Spirit. His perfect peace and love leave no room for darkness or fear to abide in it. He lifts us out of the pit of darkness and into His glorious light!

Reflect:

How is your heart? Have you asked God to clean it up? Are you willing to do the work to get rid of anything that may be in it that is not from Him?

Pray:

Heavenly Father, thank you for the healing work You have done in my heart. May I remain centered and focused on You by seeking You first in all I do. May I always have a healthy and strong heart that represents You with pure motives, and is guided by Your love and peace. In Jesus' name, I pray. Amen.

Declare:

My heart is filled with God's love.

I am thankful for...

_____

_____

_____

_____

_____

Prayer Requests...

_____

_____

_____

_____

_____

What is God's Word saying to you today?...

_____

_____

_____

_____

_____

_____

Make the Most of Your Gift

"We have different gifts according to the grace given to each of us. If your gift is prophesying, then prophesy in accordance with your faith; if it is serving, then serve; if it is teaching, then teach; if it is to encourage, then give encouragement; if it is giving, then give generously; if it is to lead, do it diligently; if it is to show mercy, do it cheerfully." - Romans 12:6-8

Resist the urge to be like others. God gave you a unique fingerprint so you can leave your own unique imprint on the things you do and the people you touch. Stay true to who He created you to be. Stay in your gift. Stay in your anointing. Stay in your authentic assignment. Choose to stay the course, and stay centered in Him. He will reveal your gift, your timing, and your path when you put your trust and faith in Him.

Reflect:

How are you sharing your gift with the world?

Pray:

Heavenly Father, thank you for making me uniquely wonderful. Help me to stay in my authentic gift so that I can live my life according to Your purpose for it. May I grow in my purpose and share the gift of who You created me to be with those You place around me. May my presence draw people closer to You. In Jesus' name, I pray. Amen.

Declare:

I am aware of my gift and I share it without limits. I chart my own course in Christ to be the best version of myself.

I am thankful for...

_____

_____

_____

_____

_____

Prayer Requests...

_____

_____

_____

_____

What is God's Word saying to you today?...

_____

_____

_____

_____

_____

_____

Be Present with People

"You make known to me the path of life; in your presence there is fullness of joy; at your right hand are pleasures forevermore." - Psalm 16:11

Be present with people when there are people in your presence. Just as there is fullness of joy in His presence, let there be fullness of joy in your presence when you are with people. When we live knowing that the greater One lives in us, we can tap into the fullness of joy that Christ offers. When we are living in Christ in this manner, His presence radiates from our innermost being to all those around us.

Reflect:

Are you present with people? Does the presence of Christ dwell in you? When people see you, do they see Him?

Pray:

Heavenly Father, when people see me, let them see You. I want to be so filled with Your presence that there is no question about who I am in the presence of others. Help me be present and centered in You as I go about my day. In Jesus' name, I pray. Amen.

Declare:

I am present with people. The fullness of joy that comes from Christ, alone, abides in me.

I am thankful for...

_____

_____

_____

_____

_____

Prayer Requests...

_____

_____

_____

_____

_____

What is God's Word saying to you today?...

_____

_____

_____

_____

_____

_____

Be Christ's Image Bearer

Love

"If you love those who love you, what benefit is that to you? For even sinners love those who love them. And if you do good to those who do good to you, what benefit is that to you? For even sinners do the same. And if you lend to those from whom you expect to receive, what credit is that to you? Even sinners lend to sinners to get back the same amount. But love your enemies, and do good, and lend, expecting nothing in return, and your reward will be great, and you will be sons of the Most High, for he is kind to the ungrateful and the evil. Be merciful, even as your Father is merciful." – Luke 6:32-36

Judge not

"Judge not, and you will not be judged; condemn not, and you will not be condemned; forgive, and you will be forgiven; give, and it will be given to you. Good measure, pressed down, shaken together, running over, will be put into your lap. For with the measure you use, it will be measured back to you." He also told them a parable: "Can a blind man lead a blind man? Will they not both fall into a pit? A disciple is not above his teacher, but everyone when he is fully trained will be like his teacher. Why do you see the speck that is in your brother's eye, but do not notice the log that is in your own eye? How can you say to your brother, 'Brother, let me take out the speck that is in your eye,' when you yourself do not see the log that is in your own eye? You hypocrite, first take the log out of your own eye, and then you will see clearly to take out the speck that is in your brother's eye." - Luke 6:37-42

How we walk in this world matters. How we treat others matters. Every day is an opportunity for us to be more Christlike in our interactions. It is most challenging to be Christlike when we are around people who challenge us the most. It is during these times that we find out a lot about ourselves. When our faith is being tested, we have the opportunity to show others who Christ is by moving past our own response and into His. When we judge not and display genuine love, we are treating others the way that God wants us to treat them. True growth in Christ results in us genuinely extending compassion and grace to those that are the most difficult to extend it to.

Reflect:

How are you treating those who challenge you most? When you are experiencing judgmental thoughts, how are you moving past them? What are some ways that you show genuine love to the people God places on your path each day?

Pray:

Heavenly Father, I want to be Your image bearer. Help me live my life according to Your ways. I need Your loving presence to shine through me, especially during the times where I find it most difficult. Help me live without judgment and be a true representative of You in all that I say and do. May others come to know You when they know me. In Jesus' name, I pray. Amen.

Declare:

I am Christ's image bearer. I choose to love more and judge less.

I am thankful for...

_____

_____

_____

_____

_____

Prayer Requests...

_____

_____

_____

_____

_____

What is God's Word saying to you today?...

_____

_____

_____

_____

_____

_____

Our Battles are His

"Thus says the Lord to you, 'Do not be afraid and do not be dismayed at this vast army, for the battle is not yours but God's.'" - 2 Chronicles 20:15

It's comforting to know that the battles we face are God's. Outwardly, in the flesh, it may appear to be painful and destructive, but inwardly, the spiritual work produces blessings. Many of our most incredible blessings were birthed from great sorrow and pain. Whenever a time of deep and painful pruning takes place, it's important to have faith, knowing that "My Father is the gardener." - John 15:1

There are many abundant blessings we will only receive through the painful path of pruning and cutting away all that doesn't produce a bountiful harvest. You have to be willing to give yourself away so He can use you. Trust that your battle belongs to the Lord, and rest in His promise of a victorious outcome.

God prunes every branch that bears fruit. Let Him prune you. Your fruit is coming.

Reflect:

How are you trusting Him in the midst of the battle? Are you doing your part and trusting Him to do His?

Pray:

Heavenly Father, thank you for being with me in the midst of the battle. I trust the outcome because I know this battle belongs to You. Your word says that we are more than conquerors in You. Thank you for bringing victory into every part of my life as I put my faith completely in You. May I continue to trust You and walk in complete obedience, regardless of what comes my way. In Jesus' name, I pray. Amen.

Declare:

I am victorious. I am more than a conqueror.

I am thankful for...

_____

_____

_____

_____

_____

Prayer Requests...

_____

_____

_____

_____

_____

What is God's Word saying to you today?...

_____

_____

_____

_____

_____

_____

You Will Succeed

"Commit to the Lord whatever you do, and he will establish your plans." - Proverbs 16:3

Each of us has a gift from God that we have been given in order to love and serve others. When God gives us a gift, He wants us to use it. He will make us strong in the areas we are weak in order to step out in faith with Him to share our gift. He will ensure His plans succeed when we choose to honor Him with our daily choices.

Reflect:

Are you committing your plans to the Lord? How are you doing so? Do you trust Him to establish your plans and purpose according to your highest calling?

Pray:

Heavenly Father, I trust You to establish my plans. I commit my ways to You, knowing that You will lead me each day down the path that You have prepared for me. You know the beginning from the end, and I trust You to lead me where You need me to go. May I always continue to walk in Your ways. In Jesus' name, I pray. Amen.

Declare:

I am successful through Christ. I commit my ways to Him.

I am thankful for...

_____

_____

_____

_____

_____

Prayer Requests...

_____

_____

_____

_____

_____

What is God's Word saying to you today?...

_____

_____

_____

_____

_____

_____

Please God, Not People

"On the contrary, we speak as those approved by God to be entrusted with the gospel. We are not trying to please people but God, who tests our hearts." - 1 Thessalonians 2:4

Our purpose is to please God, not people. The ones who are living in their purpose will be criticized, and the second they achieve something of value, they will be persecuted. If you are in God's will, that is all that truly matters. Each time you step out in faith to do what He has called you to do, there will be noise and resistance from those around you. Know who you are in Him, so that you won't be swayed by the noise.

At the end of the day, I want to know that God is pleased with me, not people.

"Whatever you do, work at it with all your heart, as working for the Lord, not for human masters, since you know that you will receive an inheritance from the Lord as a reward. It is the Lord Christ you are serving." - Colossians 3:23-24

Reflect:

How are you pleasing God? Are you worried about what people think, or are you more concerned about what God thinks?

Pray:

Heavenly Father, I want to please You. Anytime my behavior results in me trying to please people, help me see what I'm doing so that I can adjust my focus back to You. In Jesus' name, I pray. Amen.

Declare:

I am here to please God, not people.

I am thankful for...

_____

_____

_____

_____

_____

Prayer Requests...

_____

_____

_____

_____

_____

What is God's Word saying to you today?...

_____

_____

_____

_____

_____

_____

Rise up and Conquer

"Consider it pure joy, my brothers and sisters, whenever you face trials of many kinds, because you know that the testing of your faith produces perseverance. Let perseverance finish its work so that you may be mature and complete, not lacking anything." - James 1:2-4

When we face difficult situations, we are being prepared for the road ahead. When we see our obstacles and challenges in this way, we begin to understand what it means to be prepared to be more than conquerors in Him who loves us. (Romans 8:37)

The Lord is uncovering our purpose and giving us an opportunity to grow in Him. He is developing the qualities in us to become soldiers who are equipped for the battle, so we may use every gift He has given us to become more than conquerors.

Reflect:

In what ways do you find that God is preparing you in this moment to be more than a conqueror?

Pray:

Heavenly Father, I know that regardless of the challenges I face, I am more than a conqueror in You. Help me to find the joy in each day as You prepare me for my greatest purpose. In Jesus' name, I pray. Amen.

Declare:

I am more than a conqueror in Christ who loves me.

I am thankful for...

_____

_____

_____

_____

_____

Prayer Requests...

_____

_____

_____

_____

_____

What is God's Word saying to you today?...

_____

_____

_____

_____

_____

_____

Steadfast Faith

"Be on your guard; stand firm in the faith; be courageous; be strong." - 1 Corinthians 16:13

If you don't stand firm in your faith, you won't stand at all. The adversity we face in life will ultimately become an advantage for those of us who choose to keep doing what is right. We need to keep doing good no matter how we feel, and act with courage when God whispers to us. It is through suffering that the strength of our soul is developed and our greatest character exposed. Let the inside work be done through steadfast faith in the midst of the fire.

Reflect:

How are you standing firm in your faith today? Is there anything you need to do differently?

Pray:

Heavenly Father, as I do my part to be courageous and strong in what You have called me to do, I ask that You plant my feet firmly in Your ways. May I be on guard and stand firm in the faith knowing You are with me through it all. In Jesus' name, I pray. Amen.

Declare:

I am unshakable. I stand firm in the faith.

I am thankful for...

_____

_____

_____

_____

_____

Prayer Requests...

_____

_____

_____

_____

_____

What is God's Word saying to you today?...

_____

_____

_____

_____

_____

_____

Let Them Judge & Criticize You

"When they hurled their insults at him, he did not retaliate; when he suffered, he made no threats. Instead, he entrusted himself to him who judges justly." - 1 Peter 2:23

We are required to walk out Christ's love regardless of what's happening around us. One of the greatest tests of our character as a Christian is when we are judged unfairly, when something hurtful is spoken about us, yet we respond with the sweetness of the Holy Spirit. Some Christians are easily turned away from their divine calling by getting into the flesh to defend their name and battle against the lies in their own strength. Nothing good comes when we battle in the flesh and start mudslinging with the enemy. That's exactly how the enemy works to get us off our game. We win these battles through the power of the Holy Spirit, for "greater is He who is in us than he who is in the world." (1 John 4:4)

Reflect:

Are you rising above the criticism? Are you being true to your calling and purpose? What do you do in response to criticism?

Pray:

Heavenly Father, I know that I shouldn't worry about what people think. But I admit that every once in a while, I do. Help me continue to grow in You so that I can truly get to a place where the opinions of others don't bother me, because I know that You are pleased with me. Help me to no longer feel the need to defend myself against the lies of the enemy and place my trust in You who judges justly. In Jesus' name, I pray. Amen.

Declare:

I am the righteousness of God in Christ.

I am thankful for...

_____

_____

_____

_____

_____

Prayer Requests...

_____

_____

_____

_____

_____

What is God's Word saying to you today?...

_____

_____

_____

_____

_____

_____

Jesus Was Persecuted by the Crowd

"Consider him who endured such opposition from sinners, so that you will not grow weary and lose heart." - Hebrews 12:3

My son called me this morning, explaining a situation where he was treated poorly for no reason at all. We had a discussion about how we are disciples of Christ and that Jesus was persecuted by the crowd. We trust that God places us in situations to test us, to grow our faith, and to be His representatives in a world that needs to see more of Him.

Reflect:

When you encounter persecution, are you representing Christ or yourself?

Pray:

Heavenly Father, I want to represent You in every situation. Help me to do this well when I least expect to encounter the enemy. May I be so grounded in my faith and centered in You that nothing will shake me. In Jesus' name, I pray. Amen.

Declare:

I consider it pure joy when I am persecuted for His namesake.

I am thankful for...

_____

_____

_____

_____

_____

Prayer Requests...

_____

_____

_____

_____

_____

What is God's Word saying to you today?...

_____

_____

_____

_____

_____

_____

He Gently Whispers

Then He said, "Go out, and stand on the mountain before the Lord." And behold, the Lord passed by, and a great and strong wind tore into the mountains and broke the rocks in pieces before the Lord, *but* the Lord *was* not in the wind; and after the wind an earthquake, *but* the Lord *was* not in the earthquake; and after the earthquake a fire, *but* the Lord *was* not in the fire; and after the fire a still small voice. So it was, when Elijah heard *it,* that he wrapped his face in his mantle and went out and stood in the entrance of the cave. Suddenly a voice *came* to him, and said, "What are you doing here, Elijah?" - 1 Kings 19:11-13

Learn to hear His gentle whisper by seeking Him at all times. He speaks to us with his still small voice. Be still and know that God will speak to you with a gentle whisper. He speaks to us through our God-given intuition. Seek Him and you will find Him. Ask and He will answer. Trust and He will deliver on His promises. When the noise of the world is loud, go to a quiet place within so you can hear His gentle whisper.

Reflect:

Are you hearing from God? Do you have time in your day that is quiet and calm? How can you find more time to be still so you can focus on hearing His gentle whisper?

Pray:

Heavenly Father, I want to always have time to be in a place where I can hear directly from You. I know that I can become distracted with the busyness of the day, which tends to take my focus off of You. Help me to notice those times during the day that I become distracted so that I can quickly return to hearing Your gentle whisper in the midst of all the noise. In Jesus' name, I pray. Amen.

Declare:

I know and hear God's voice. (John 10:14)

I am thankful for...

_____

_____

_____

_____

_____

Prayer Requests...

_____

_____

_____

_____

_____

What is God's Word saying to you today?...

_____

_____

_____

_____

_____

_____

Sow in Faith

"Bring the whole tithe into the storehouse, so that there may be food in My house, and test Me now in this," says the LORD of hosts, "if I will not open for you the windows of heaven and pour out for you a blessing until it overflows." - Malachi 3:10

Giving and sowing in faith, based on the divine principle that everything we have comes from God's hands, will lead us to reap an abundant harvest. We must first have faith in our seed, for if we sow our seed in faith, we know we will reap a bountiful harvest.

Galatians 6:9 says, "So let's not allow ourselves to get fatigued doing good. At the right time, we will harvest a good crop if we don't give up, or quit."

Reflect:

How are you sowing a seed in faith? Are you giving generously? In what ways can you expand your giving to honor and glorify the Lord? In what ways are you holding back?

Pray:

Heavenly Father, I want to give abundantly to all of the causes that You place on my heart. Help me be in a position where I can give to every good cause without having to worry about not having the resources to do so. In Jesus' name, I pray. Amen.

Declare:

I give generously to every good cause the Lord places on my heart.

I am thankful for...

_____

_____

_____

_____

_____

Prayer Requests...

_____

_____

_____

_____

What is God's Word saying to you today?...

_____

_____

_____

_____

_____

Encourage Yourself

"And David was greatly distressed; for the people spoke of stoning him, because the soul of all the people was grieved, every man for his sons and for his daughters: but David encouraged himself in the Lord his God." - 1 Samuel 30:6

Have you been greatly distressed lately? Sometimes, we get to a place where we are exhausted and worn out. During these times of distress, we need to encourage ourselves to keep going. We need to stop and seek strength from God. How do we do that? I take time each morning and throughout the day to read scripture, listen to faith-based messages and worship music, and find simple ways to rest throughout the day in His presence. In the midst of a busy day, I often pause within to pray and access the power of the Holy Spirit.

Reflect:

How are you encouraging yourself?

Pray:

Heavenly Father, when I am distressed and discouraged, thank You for always being right there with me. Thank you for being my peace and strength. You are my encourager and source of hope. May I live my life knowing that You, the greater One, lives in me. In Jesus' name, I pray. Amen.

Declare:

I encourage myself in Christ.

I am thankful for...

_____

_____

_____

_____

_____

Prayer Requests...

_____

_____

_____

_____

_____

What is God's Word saying to you today?...

_____

_____

_____

_____

_____

Heartfelt Prayer

"And when you pray, do not keep on babbling like pagans, for they think they will be heard because of their many words. Do not be like them, for your Father knows what you need before you ask him." - Matthew 6:7-8

Effective prayer is a simple, heartfelt conversation with God. A simple prayer that I say often is, "Jesus, I need you." God answers our simple, earnest prayers. He loves our sincerity, belief, and unwavering faith in Him. Whatever it is that we need, we can ask Him for it and He will provide for us. The time spent with God in our day-to-day activities increases our intimacy with him. He loves to answer our prayers. "Draw near to God and He will draw near to you." - James 4:8

Reflect:

Are your prayers sincere? How can you improve your prayer life?

Pray:

Heavenly Father, I am so grateful to be known and loved by You. I want my prayer life to flow and become an integral part of who I am. I want to be in constant fellowship with You. I need You in the daily details of my life. In Jesus' name, I pray. Amen.

Declare:

I am in constant fellowship with God. He is my source.

I am thankful for...

_____

_____

_____

_____

_____

Prayer Requests...

_____

_____

_____

_____

_____

What is God's Word saying to you today?...

_____

_____

_____

_____

_____

_____

Trust the Season You're in

"I would have lost heart unless I believed." - Psalm 27:13

Life can be overwhelming at times. I have been in a place lately where my eyes are fixed on the promises of God. I would be completely disheartened if I could only see the ways of the world through my own eyes. I'm so grateful that I know God and that He's given me the ability to see according to my faith and the promises of His Word. I have been in a season of painful, yet beautiful, preparation as I wait upon the Lord. He is showing me during this season that He is with me, and that this is all necessary preparation for what's to come. He's developing me in this hiding place for what He's about to bring to pass. He's using my circumstances to prepare me for the platform that will glorify His name mightily in all ways. The storm is my training ground, and He is with me in the midst of it all.

Reflect:

How are you trusting God during this season? Is your mind fixed on Him?

Pray:

Heavenly Father, I trust You and know that You are working in my life, even when I can't see or feel it. Thank You for giving me a renewed sense of hope during this season of painful preparation. Help me stay centered in You. Help me release the need to try to control the outcome. In Jesus' name, I pray. Amen.

Declare:

I trust the season I am in. I know God is working in my life right now.

I am thankful for...

_____

_____

_____

_____

_____

Prayer Requests...

_____

_____

_____

_____

_____

What is God's Word saying to you today?...

_____

_____

_____

_____

_____

_____

Live with Integrity

"The righteous man walks in his integrity; His children are blessed after him." - Proverbs 20:7

"The integrity of the upright will guide them, but the crookedness of the treacherous will destroy them." - Proverbs 11:3

Never compromise your character or convictions for the comfort of others. Expect distractors. Ignore the noise. Trust God to protect you and your reputation. Don't stop to explain yourself. God knows your motives, and that is what matters most. Keep moving forward and don't look back. Do the next right thing and keep doing the good He has called you to do, regardless of how you feel.

Reflect:

How are you living with integrity? Do your actions match your words? Are you consistent in who you are on the inside with how you present yourself on the outside? What is an area that you can grow in to be a more consistent person of integrity?

Pray:

Heavenly Father, I want who I am on the inside to be magnified on the outside. Thank you for working on my innermost being, so that Your reflection is what people see outwardly. Help me be more like You. In Jesus' name, I pray. Amen.

Declare:

I live with integrity.

I am thankful for...

_____

_____

_____

_____

_____

Prayer Requests...

_____

_____

_____

_____

_____

What is God's Word saying to you today?...

_____

_____

_____

_____

_____

_____

Be the Change

"Finally, be strong in the Lord and in his mighty power."
- Ephesians 6:10

Let God change you so you can then change the world around you by how you walk out the truth of His love in your daily life. Let your life be a living example of His truth and love to all who cross your path. Be transformed by the word of God, and in doing so, be the change the world so desperately needs to see.

Do everything you can, every day, as often as possible, to add value to the lives of others. By doing all the good you can in all the ways you can, you will be one of those rare people who makes the world a better place for others.

Reflect:

What are you doing to bring forth positive change? How are you walking out the truth of His love in your daily life?

Pray:

Heavenly Father, I believe that we must be the change we wish to see. Help me live my life as a representative of the change You wish to see, and by doing so, influence others to do the same. In Jesus' name, I pray. Amen.

Declare:

I am strong in the Lord and am a living expression of His truth and love.

I am thankful for...

_____

_____

_____

_____

_____

Prayer Requests...

_____

_____

_____

_____

_____

What is God's Word saying to you today?...

_____

_____

_____

_____

_____

_____

Pray Without Ceasing

"Pray continually, give thanks in all circumstances; for this is God's will for you in Christ Jesus." - 1 Thessalonians 5:17-18

Understanding what it means to pray without ceasing has been a process for me. I used to think prayer was something that other people needed and would view it as a weakness if I needed it. When I came to the end of myself through my brokenness and cried out to God for help, that is when my understanding of prayer began to grow and develop. I sought out prayer from others until I began to realize the power of prayer through the Holy Spirit was within me. Now prayer is a more natural part of my daily walk. I do my best to pray my way through my day.

Reflect:

Do you pray? How do you pray? What does prayer mean to you?

Pray:

Heavenly Father, I want to be in constant communion with You. I know that You are my source for every bit of my purpose in this world, and that in order to live according to Your plans for my highest purpose, I need to pray my way through the day. Please help me stay on the path that You have for me. Help me stay centered in You so that the noise of this world doesn't distract me from my divine purpose. In Jesus' name, I pray. Amen.

Declare:

I am a prayer warrior. I pray without ceasing.

I am thankful for...

_____

_____

_____

_____

_____

Prayer Requests...

_____

_____

_____

_____

_____

What is God's Word saying to you today?...

_____

_____

_____

_____

_____

_____

I Am Who He Says I Am

"No weapon formed against you shall prosper, and every tongue which rises against you in judgment You shall condemn. This is the heritage of the servants of the Lord, and their righteousness is from Me," says the Lord." - Isaiah 54:17

Weapons formed against you won't be successful. In fact, they may appear to be working, but the outcome will be the exact opposite. God will use those attacks to justify and elevate you. He will use your situation to glorify Him. Even Jesus was falsely accused. We know that Satan is a liar, and when you are committed to doing God's will, the enemy will attack you. When you give the battle to God and leave it in His hands, He will vindicate you. This battle will become another testimony of how good, mighty and faithful our God truly is.

Reflect:

What is your first thought when you see a weapon being formed against you? How do you respond and where do you turn? Do you trust God with the outcome? Do you give the enemy room to prosper?

Pray:

Heavenly Father, I trust You with the outcome of every battle I face. I know that weapons will be formed against me and that my feelings might waiver, but I know that no matter what I'm going through, I'm going through it with You. Help me be strong in the midst of the battle. Help me not take it personally. Give me the strength to know that every battle I face is ultimately to glorify You. I am who You say I am. In Jesus' name, I pray. Amen.

Declare:

I am not who the enemy says I am. I am who God says I am.

I am thankful for...

_____

_____

_____

_____

_____

Prayer Requests...

_____

_____

_____

_____

_____

What is God's Word saying to you today?...

_____

_____

_____

_____

_____

New and Sharp

"Behold, I will make thee a new sharp threshing instrument having teeth: thou shalt thresh the mountains, and beat them small, and shalt make the hills as chaff." - Isaiah 41:15

He makes us new and sharp. The more we are shaped by the fire, beaten, pounded, and polished through life's trials, the greater value we have to minister to others in this world. It is through our pain and suffering that God gets the most out of us for His glory. The sharper the craftsmanship, the more beautiful is his work.

Reflect:

How are you allowing God to craft you? Are you willingly presenting yourself to Him for His purpose? Are you living according to your purpose in Christ?

Pray:

Heavenly Father, sometimes I don't understand what it is that You are doing. I trust that as long as I stay in a humble place with You, You will truly work everything together for the good, of not only me, but more importantly Your kingdom. I need You to keep me on the path that You have for me. Help me battle the enemy that is trying to pull me away and take me down as I move forward with You. In Jesus' name, I pray. Amen.

Declare:

I am a new and sharp instrument for Christ.

I am thankful for...

_____

_____

_____

_____

_____

Prayer Requests...

_____

_____

_____

_____

_____

What is God's Word saying to you today?...

_____

_____

_____

_____

_____

_____

Be Still and Know

"Be still, and know that I am God; I will be exalted among the nations, I will be exalted in the earth." - Psalm 46:10

When someone mistreats you, it's a character-building opportunity to grow in grace. Make it a habit to learn to be peaceful as you put your trust in God in every situation. There is tremendous power available to us when we are still and silent, living in complete faith in God.

Reflect:

How are you carving out time to be still and silent with God each day?

Pray:

Heavenly Father, sometimes it's hard for me to be still and know that You are working. I trust the plans You have for me. In my weakness, help me to know when I need to do my part and when I need to be still and trust in You to do your part. Thank you for loving me through it all, as I take refuge and rest in You. In Jesus' name, I pray. Amen.

Declare:

I know there is tremendous power in stillness. When I am still, I am strong.

I am thankful for...

_____

_____

_____

_____

_____

Prayer Requests...

_____

_____

_____

_____

What is God's Word saying to you today?...

_____

_____

_____

_____

_____

Seek Wisdom & Discernment

"For the Lord gives wisdom; from His mouth come knowledge and understanding. He holds success in store for the upright, He is a shield to those who walk with integrity." - Proverbs 2:6-7

"But the wisdom that comes from heaven is first of all pure; then peace-loving, considerate, submissive, full of mercy and good fruit, impartial and sincere. Peacemakers who sow in peace reap a harvest of righteousness." - James 3:17-18

"If any of you lacks wisdom, you should ask God, who gives generously to all without finding fault, and it will be given to you. But when you ask, you must believe and not doubt, because the one who doubts is like a wave of the sea, blown and tossed by the wind. That person should not expect to receive anything from the Lord. Such a person is double-minded and unstable in all they do." - James 1:5-8

"The fear of the Lord is the beginning of wisdom; all who follow His precepts have good understanding. To Him belongs eternal praise." - Psalm 111:10

"Give me wisdom and knowledge, that I may lead this people, for who is able to govern this great people of yours?" - 2 Chronicles 1:10

I need to pursue Godly wisdom. Instead of going to others or trying to figure things out in my own strength, I need to get in the habit of going to Him. Studying the Bible, getting in His word and meditating on it. Spending alone time with Him leads to growth in godly wisdom and discernment.

Reflect:

Are you trying to figure things out on your own? When you're lacking in wisdom or discernment, do you go to people or do you go straight to God? How can you grow in this area?

Pray:

Heavenly Father, I want to be wise as I walk about this world. I want to seek You for wisdom and study Your word so that there's less of a chance for me to be deceived. Help me grow in this area of truly seeking your guidance in all that I do. In Jesus' name, I pray. Amen.

Declare:

I diligently seek wisdom and discernment from God.

I am thankful for...

_____

_____

_____

_____

_____

Prayer Requests...

_____

_____

_____

_____

_____

What is God's Word saying to you today?...

_____

_____

_____

_____

_____

_____

Put on Love

"Put on then, as God's chosen ones, holy and beloved, compassionate hearts, kindness, humility, meekness, and patience, bearing with one another, and if one has a complaint against another, forgiving each other; as the Lord has forgiven you, so you also must forgive. And above all these put on love, which binds everything together in perfect harmony. And let the peace of Christ rule in your hearts, to which indeed you were called in one body. And be thankful."
- Colossians 3:12-15

In order to be able to put on love, we need to know what love is. Put your name in every place that love shows up in the following passage. This is what it means to put on God's love.

"Love is patient, love is kind. It does not envy, it does not boast, it is not proud. It does not dishonor others, it is not self-seeking, it is not easily angered, it keeps no record of wrongs. Love does not delight in evil but rejoices with the truth. It always protects, always trusts, always hopes, always perseveres." - 1 Corinthians 13:4-7

Reflect:

What does it look like in your life when you intentionally choose to put on love? When you put your name in the above passage, do you notice any areas that are strong and any areas that are weak when it comes to your ability to put on love? What are you going to do today to put on love and grow in your daily love walk?

Pray:

Heavenly Father, help me love others well. I want to love the way that You love. Thank you for being the most amazing example of what love truly is. Before I knew You, I had no idea what it meant to love or be loved. I need Your help as I grow in my daily love walk. Place people on my path that you want me to show the goodness of Your love to. In Jesus' name, I pray. Amen.

Declare:

I choose to put on God's love every day.

I am thankful for...

_____

_____

_____

_____

_____

Prayer Requests...

_____

_____

_____

_____

_____

What is God's Word saying to you today?...

_____

_____

_____

_____

_____

_____

Enjoy Today

"I will instruct you and teach you in the way you should go; I will counsel you and watch over you." - Psalm 32:8

Beginning my day alone with God is what matters most when it comes to how my day goes. Being still in His presence equips me for the day ahead. He keeps me from growing weary and losing heart. He is my hope and strength. He is my comforter and protector. He leads me beside still waters and restores my soul. (Psalm 23:1-6)

Reflect:

As you go about your day, how are you taking the time to notice the path that God has you on? Are you noticing the people He places on that path? Are you slowing down enough to be connected to His spirit that is living in you?

Pray:

Heavenly Father, lead the way. Show me what You need me to do today and give me the courage to do it. In Jesus' name, I pray. Amen.

Declare:

I am led by God. He directs my steps.

I am thankful for...

_____

_____

_____

_____

_____

Prayer Requests...

_____

_____

_____

_____

_____

What is God's Word saying to you today?...

_____

_____

_____

_____

_____

_____

People Will Come Against You

"Consider him who endured such opposition from sinful men, so that you will not grow weary and lose heart." - Hebrews 12:3

Overcome evil with good. Regardless of what people are doing around you, or what they are doing to you, continue to do the good that God has called you to do. Jesus did not offer insult back, instead He asked His father to forgive them for they know not what they do. May we be more like Jesus as we interact with others. May we consider Him and everything He endured for us, so that we will not grow weary or lose heart. May we keep doing the next right thing for His namesake.

Reflect:

What do you do when you grow weary? When you begin to lose heart, how do you keep going?

Pray:

Heavenly Father, I know that I need to rest when I'm tired and weary. Thank you for providing me with opportunities to rest in You each and every day. Help me learn to draw upon Your strength when I am growing weary. When I grow weary and tired, help me continue to do good and not lose heart. In Jesus' name, I pray. Amen.

Declare:

I am strong in the Lord.

I am thankful for...

_____

_____

_____

_____

_____

Prayer Requests...

_____

_____

_____

_____

_____

What is God's Word saying to you today?...

_____

_____

_____

_____

_____

_____

Lift Others Up

"Let each one of us make it a practice to please (make happy) his neighbor for his good and for his true welfare, to edify him [to strengthen him and build him up spiritually.]" - Romans 15:2

The word of God calls us to lift one another up, esteeming others more highly than ourselves. (Philippians 2:3)

We need to avoid people who constantly criticize others and spend our time, instead, with those who live in service to lift others up. Our time and energy is best spent doing God's work with uplifting people who are committed to doing the same.

Reflect:

How are you lifting others up? How are you doing God's work?

Pray:

Heavenly Father, I am committed to lifting others up and leading them to You. Thank you for loving me the way that You do. It is through Your love that I know how to love. Lead me and show me how to lift others up. I want to represent You well in all that I say and do. In Jesus' name, I pray. Amen.

Declare:

I lift others up.

I am thankful for...

_____

_____

_____

_____

_____

Prayer Requests...

_____

_____

_____

_____

_____

What is God's Word saying to you today?...

_____

_____

_____

_____

_____

_____

The Spirit Works for Us

"In the same way, the Spirit helps us in our weakness. We do not know what we ought to pray for, but the Spirit Himself intercedes for us through wordless groans. And he who searches our hearts knows the mind of the Spirit, because the Spirit intercedes for God's people in accordance with the will of God." - Romans 8:26-27

I'm so grateful that the Spirit intercedes for me regardless of what I'm facing. When I don't know what to pray, the Spirit knows and prays on my behalf. When I'm not sure where to go or what to say, the Spirit knows. I am so thankful that I can trust that my steps are ordered by God and the Spirit is working in and through me at all times. Even when I can't feel it or understand in the moment what is happening, God has ordained the very moment that I'm in. He is working with the Spirit that lives in me to bring His will to pass in my life.

Reflect:

What does this passage mean to you? Have you experienced the Spirit working on your behalf in your life?

Pray:

Heavenly Father, I earnestly want to be connected with the Spirit at all times. I know You know this, because my prayers through the Spirit have been communicated with You often. May this prayer be one that is between You and the Spirit that lives in me. In Jesus' name, I pray. Amen.

Declare:

His Spirit lives in me and leads me to higher ground.

I am thankful for...

_____

_____

_____

_____

_____

Prayer Requests...

_____

_____

_____

_____

_____

What is God's Word saying to you today?...

_____

_____

_____

_____

_____

_____

You Are God's Masterpiece

"For we are God's masterpiece. He has created us anew in Christ Jesus, so we can do the good things He planned for us long ago." - Ephesians 2:10

No matter what has happened, if you seek God with all your heart, He will restore you to the masterpiece that He created you to be in His image. He has created you anew in Christ Jesus, so let His bright light shine in and through you. When the eyes of another person meet yours, let His light touch their heart in that very moment. You are His masterpiece and your presence blesses people.

Reflect:

When people see you, do they see Him? How can you be more intentional in blessing people with His presence each day?

Pray:

Heavenly Father, thank you for creating me anew in Your image. Help me to see that I am Your masterpiece, especially when I don't feel like I am. May I get so busy doing the good things You planned for me long ago that I forget about myself as I get lost in You. In Jesus' name, I pray. Amen.

Declare:

I am God's masterpiece.

I am thankful for...

_____

_____

_____

_____

_____

Prayer Requests...

_____

_____

_____

_____

_____

What is God's Word saying to you today?...

_____

_____

_____

_____

_____

_____

Desires of Your Heart

"Delight yourself in the Lord and he will give you the desires of your heart." - Psalm 37:4

To delight yourself in the Lord means to exalt Him so highly that you pursue Him over any other person, thing, thought, or action in your life, especially those things that would keep Him from being in first place.

I have this written in my home as a daily reminder, "I only chase God, and as a result, His abundant blessings and favor chase me down and overtake me." Every good and perfect gift comes from God, and I want to be sure He is always in His proper place in my life.

Reflect:

How are you delighting yourself in the Lord? How are you keeping Him in his proper place?

Pray:

Heavenly Father, You are the only one who can satisfy my heart. I need You every hour of every day. Lately, I've been feeling weak. I know in my weakness, You are strong. I look to You this morning as I prepare for the day. I know You will lead the way as I seek Your will and not my own. Your will is what my heart desires most. In Jesus' name, I pray. Amen.

Declare:

God gives me the desires of my heart, because I delight myself in Him. I only chase God, and as a result, His abundant blessings and favor chase me down and overtake me.

I am thankful for...

_____

_____

_____

_____

_____

Prayer Requests...

_____

_____

_____

_____

What is God's Word saying to you today?...

_____

_____

_____

_____

_____

Joyful Spirit

"The joy of the Lord is your strength." - Nehemiah 8:10

You shine differently when God is at the center of your heart. Life's troubles can never rob us of the joy God gives us, as we turn in faith to Him and seek His face to shine upon us. True joy radiates from within our hearts and makes its presence known regardless of what we are going through. When we are living in the beauty of our authentic joy, it shows. Let's be less concerned about appearances and more concerned about who we really are.

Reflect:

Are you open to receiving strength from the Lord? How are you preparing yourself to represent His joyful spirit today?

Pray:

Heavenly Father, give me the strength today to be mindful and present and totally represent Your joy to those in my presence. When they see me, let them see You. In Jesus' name, I pray. Amen.

Declare:

The joy of the Lord is my strength.

I am thankful for...

_____

_____

_____

_____

_____

Prayer Requests...

_____

_____

_____

_____

_____

What is God's Word saying to you today?...

_____

_____

_____

_____

_____

_____

You Are Called

"The gifts and calling of God are irrevocable." - Romans 11:29

God doesn't take back the gifts He has given or abandon the people He has chosen. Develop your gifts. Trust the Lord and take a step in faith as you walk in and toward your purpose. He has placed your gifts on the inside of you and He wants to help you develop them. Our gifts are a blessing. Never be satisfied with being anything less than the very best you can be. God has great plans for your life, so let go of the past and step boldly into the future, keeping your eyes fixed on Him and what lies ahead.

"God has given us different gifts." - Romans 12:6

Reflect:

Are you developing the gifts God gave you? How are you using your gifts to bless others?

Pray:

Heavenly Father, I want to develop my gifts throughout life to glorify and honor Your name. Help me remove distractions so that I can be more intentional about answering Your calling in my everyday interactions with others. In Jesus' name, I pray. Amen.

Declare:

I am developing my spiritual gifts and walking in my God-ordained purpose.

I am thankful for...

_____

_____

_____

_____

_____

Prayer Requests...

_____

_____

_____

_____

What is God's Word saying to you today?...

_____

_____

_____

_____

_____

Your Word Lights My Path

"How sweet are your words to my taste, sweeter than honey to my mouth! I gain understanding from your precepts; therefore I hate every wrong path. Your word is a lamp for my feet, a light on my path." - Psalm 119:103-105

The truth of His word is so incredibly refreshing. I have been a truth seeker my entire life. I am grateful I have found it in the Bible. I had no idea for so long where to turn to, other than my own understanding, for the truth. It's all right there, and completely alive, as I read the words in the Bible. It's as though they are freshly written for each experience we go through. In the spirit, the word of God is alive, and works to transform us as we read it.

Reflect:

How does the word of God light your path?

Pray:

Heavenly Father, Your word lights my path in ways that only my heart understands. When I'm barely able to hold on, Your word somehow gives me just enough peace and strength to keep moving forward in and with You. Thank you for lighting my path. Give me strength to continue to read, speak, and trust Your word regardless of how I feel. In Jesus' name, I pray. Amen.

Declare:

I am transformed by the word of God. His word lights my path.

I am thankful for...

_____

_____

_____

_____

_____

Prayer Requests...

_____

_____

_____

_____

What is God's Word saying to you today?...

_____

_____

_____

_____

_____

Experience His Peace

"And the peace of God, which surpasses all understanding, will guard your hearts and your minds in Christ Jesus." - Philippians 4:7

In the Bible, God tells us to hold our peace and not be moved when our adversaries come against us. We are to remain constant, courageous, and at peace. We are to cast down fear and walk in faith, keeping our eyes fixed on Him. We are to hold our peace, because peace is the place of power. No matter what is happening, do your best to remain consistent and treat people well. Walk in the fruit of the Spirit. What comes out of us when we are squeezed is what's inside of us. What kind of fruit do you bear? You'll find out the answer to this question when you are facing an opponent and are in the thick of battle.

Peace I leave with you; My [perfect] peace I give to you; not as the world gives do I give to you. Do not let your heart be troubled, nor let it be afraid. [Let My perfect peace calm you in every circumstance and give you courage and strength for every challenge.] - John 14:27 (AMP)

Reflect:

Are you experiencing His peace? When do you feel the most peace? When do you feel the least amount of peace? Is there anything you need to do differently to experience more peace?

Pray:

Heavenly Father, thank you for offering Your perfect peace in every situation I face. Your peace surpasses all understanding and for that I am thankful. May I continue to turn to You and receive Your perfect peace as I put my trust in You. In Jesus' name, I pray. Amen.

Declare:

I am at peace in every situation I face.

I am thankful for...

_____

_____

_____

_____

_____

Prayer Requests...

_____

_____

_____

_____

What is God's Word saying to you today?...

_____

_____

_____

_____

_____

God Chose You

"For I have chosen him, so that he will direct his children and his household after him to keep the way of the Lord by doing what is right and just, so that the Lord will bring about for Abraham what he has promised him." - Genesis 18:19

God chooses people He can depend on. He is looking for people who will remain steadfast in faith, and people He can put weight on to carry out His work regardless of the circumstances. God continues to train and prepare us with the trials we face. May we learn our lessons and stand firm with Him. God will give us trials, and He will also give us the strength to endure and overcome them. We are more than conquerors in and through Him.

Reflect:

Can God depend on you to do what is just and right? In times of pain and adversity, how do you put your trust in Him?

Pray:

Heavenly Father, thank you for choosing us to lead our children and household after You. As we go into the week, give us strength and guidance to lead well in the midst of adversity. Place Your hedge of protection around us in a way that brings a sense of calm and security, knowing we can rest in You because You have us covered. May we do what is right and just according to Your kingdom ways by placing all of our trust in You. May You bring us victory as we move forward in life with You. In Jesus' name, I pray. Amen.

Declare:

I am God's chosen one.

I am thankful for...

_____

_____

_____

_____

_____

Prayer Requests...

_____

_____

_____

_____

_____

What is God's Word saying to you today?...

_____

_____

_____

_____

_____

_____

Hold Your Peace

"The Lord will fight for you, and you shall hold your peace."
- Exodus 14:14

Be still and know that the Lord himself is fighting for you. He will never leave you, nor forsake you. Go forth confidently, trusting and believing that the Lord is fighting for you, even when it doesn't appear that He is. Do not trust what you see, hear, or feel. His ways are higher and cannot be understood by our mind alone. We must look with our heart and trust the Holy Spirit to guide us, as we walk with our head held high, keeping our eyes fixed on Jesus and His promises.

Reflect:

How are you trusting God during this season? What do you do each day to keep your eyes fixed on Him?

Pray:

Heavenly Father, I know You will fight for me. Help me learn to be still and trust in You regardless of what is happening around me. Give me a renewed hope and a strong sense of Your peace during this season. Thank you for guiding me each day as I keep my eyes fixed on You. In Jesus' name, I pray. Amen.

Declare:

I keep my eyes fixed on Him and His promises, and He gives me peace and joy.

I am thankful for...

_____

_____

_____

_____

_____

Prayer Requests...

_____

_____

_____

_____

What is God's Word saying to you today?...

_____

_____

_____

_____

_____

Armor Up

"Therefore put on the full armor of God, so that when the day of evil comes, you may be able to stand your ground, and after you have done everything, to stand. Stand firm then, with the belt of truth buckled around your waist, with the breastplate of righteousness in place, and with your feet fitted with the readiness that comes from the gospel of peace. In addition to all this, take up the shield of faith, with which you can extinguish all the flaming arrows of the evil one. Take the helmet of salvation and the sword of the Spirit, which is the word of God. And pray in the Spirit on all occasions with all kinds of prayers and requests. With this in mind, be alert and always keep on praying for all the Lord's people." - Ephesians 6:13-18

Do the right thing and after having done all, stand. Everything that you need to do when you're facing challenging times in life is written in the Bible. This piece of scripture is one that prepares us for the challenges we face with clear guidance on how to completely armor up. We tend to want to prepare in different ways, but this is the best way to prepare for life's battles. When the day of evil comes, know that we are more than conquerors through Christ who loves us. (Romans 8:37)

Reflect:

How do you prepare for a battle? Do you even have battles? What was the most recent battle you've had and how did you fight? Did you do it in your own strength or with God?

Pray:

Heavenly Father, I don't like battles. I know that in order to become more like You, I need to experience them. Help me respond in a Christlike manner when everything in me is having a hard time doing so. I need You, Lord, to be my strength in the midst of the battle. I can't do this on my own and I know that You never meant for me to even try to do it on my own. Thank you, God, for being my strength when I am weak. In Jesus' name, I pray. Amen.

Declare:

I am armored up and ready for battle in Christ.

I am thankful for...

_____

_____

_____

_____

_____

Prayer Requests...

_____

_____

_____

_____

_____

What is God's Word saying to you today?...

_____

_____

_____

_____

_____

_____

Love Like Jesus

"He must increase, but I must decrease." - John 3:30

It can be so hard to put our feelings aside, especially when people can be so hurtful. It is in these times that we can turn to scripture and read about how Jesus was treated by "religious" people. His response in the midst of His tremendous pain and suffering was to say, "Father, forgive them, for they know not what they do." (Luke 23:34)

He knew they would hurt Him, yet He loved and forgave them anyway.

Reflect:

How can you be more like Jesus today?

Pray:

Heavenly Father, I want to be more like You. Thank you for this painful preparation. I know You see my broken heart and are comforting me during this time of transformation where You are shaping me into someone who is more like You. Help me to be loving and kind in the midst of my pain. Heal my broken heart and bind up my wounds. In Jesus' name, I pray. Amen.

Declare:

I am becoming more like Christ each day.

I am thankful for...

_____

_____

_____

_____

_____

Prayer Requests...

_____

_____

_____

_____

_____

What is God's Word saying to you today?...

_____

_____

_____

_____

_____

_____

He Is Working

"Answer me when I call to you, my righteous God, give me relief from my distress; have mercy on me and hear my prayer." - Psalm 4:1

God is working behind the scenes to answer our prayers. Trust and believe that He is working to answer your prayers. In Matthew 7:7, he states, "Ask and it will be given to you; seek and you will find; knock and the door will be opened to you." What it doesn't state is when. That's the part where our belief, trust, and faith come in. We must do all and stand tall. Waiting in this way gives us the opportunity to grow in our relationship with Him. He's at work and He will bring the desires of our heart to pass.

Reflect:

How are you waiting on Him? Do you believe He is working in your life right now?

Pray:

Heavenly Father, when I'm feeling weary and need Your strength, remind me who I am in Christ. Thank you for guiding my steps so I can overcome everything that is standing in the way of the life You have for me. In Jesus' name, I pray. Amen.

Declare:

God is for me. He is on my side, and I can do all things through Christ who strengthens me!

I am thankful for...

_____

_____

_____

_____

_____

Prayer Requests...

_____

_____

_____

_____

_____

What is God's Word saying to you today?...

_____

_____

_____

_____

_____

_____

Celebrate Often

"The Lord bless you and keep you; the Lord make His face to shine upon you and be gracious to you; the Lord lift up his countenance upon you and give you peace." - Numbers 6:24-26

We need to take time to be thankful and to celebrate along the journey. Celebration revives and restores us. Even when life is hard, we need to be grateful and celebrate the good parts. Every good gift is from God and He wants us to rejoice in Him with a grateful heart.

Reflect:

Have you taken time to celebrate anything lately? Do you stop and rejoice in the Lord? Do you have a grateful heart?

Pray:

Heavenly Father, I know that it's important to celebrate and rejoice in You. Please help me do this when the days are hard and I feel stuck in a pit of depression. Lift me higher as I keep my eyes on You. In Jesus' name, I pray. Amen.

Declare:

I am blessed because the Lord's face shines upon me.

I am thankful for...

_____

_____

_____

_____

_____

Prayer Requests...

_____

_____

_____

_____

_____

What is God's Word saying to you today?...

_____

_____

_____

_____

_____

_____

He Is at Work Within Us

"Now to him who is able to do immeasurably more than all we ask or imagine, according to his power that is at work within us." - Ephesians 3:20

Sometimes we have to go into a dark room to be fully developed in Christ. Something wonderful happens when we are in a dark place if we can stay centered in our faith. He is as work within us and His work is always to prosper and grow us. We need to stay in faith and trust the process. Don't try to rush what God is doing. His timing is better than anything we could ever hope for. We may not understand now what He is doing, but when the time comes, we will be grateful we continued to press in as He did the necessary work to grow us in His image.

"What I tell you in the dark, speak in the daylight; what is whispered in your ear, proclaim from the roofs." - Matthew 10:27

Reflect:

Have you been in a dark place lately? How is this place developing you into the best version of yourself in Christ?

Pray:

Heavenly Father, I know You are at work within me. Thank you for drawing me back to You, so that I may abide in Your presence. Thank you for loving me through my pain and suffering. Thank you for never leaving nor forsaking me. Please continue to give me the strength that I need to face each moment of each and every day. With You at work within me, I believe all things are possible. In Jesus' name, I pray. Amen.

Declare:

He is at work within me.

I am thankful for...

_____

_____

_____

_____

_____

Prayer Requests...

_____

_____

_____

_____

_____

What is God's Word saying to you today?...

_____

_____

_____

_____

_____

_____

Find Your Purpose

"Create in me a pure heart, O God, and renew a steadfast spirit within me." - Psalm 51:10

Becoming who God created you to be will be painful and hard. Choose to press into what's painful and hard anyway. When life doesn't make sense, He does. Choose faith, hope, and love. In choosing Him, you will discover your purpose and that it is worth every bit of the pain and suffering you will go through. How do you find your purpose? You can start by getting out in the world and being a blessing to others, regardless of how you feel. Be intentional about adding value and doing good every day especially on those days where you are feeling weak. That is where God does His best work in and through us, for His power is made perfect in our weakness.

Reflect:

Do you know your purpose? How can you walk in it more closely with God today? How have you experienced His power being made perfect in your weakness?

Pray:

Heavenly Father, I know You do some of Your best work in the dark. Thank you for bringing me into Your presence when I may not want to go through, what I'm going through, because it is hard and painful. Your presence is what I desire most, and I thank You for loving me enough to bring me to You for a divine encounter. Help me learn, grow and find even more clarity in my purpose as I walk this out in faith with You. In Jesus' name, I pray. Amen.

Declare:

I am walking confidently in my purpose.

I am thankful for...

_____

_____

_____

_____

_____

Prayer Requests...

_____

_____

_____

_____

_____

What is God's Word saying to you today?...

_____

_____

_____

_____

_____

_____

Listen to His Voice, His Gentle Whisper

"Whether you turn to the right or to the left, your ears will hear a voice behind you, saying, "This is the way; walk in it."
- Isaiah 30:21

His voice shows us the true way. It's important that we hear the Holy Spirit and recognize the ways He is speaking and working through us. Jesus said, "He who has ears [to hear], let him be listening and let him consider and perceive and comprehend by hearing" (Matthew 13:9). Pray that God will give you a hearing heart to listen, obey, and walk His path by walking in His ways.

It takes time to learn to discern God's voice. It also takes a humble heart that is earnestly seeking His will. The Bible tells us, "Then you will call upon Me and go and pray to Me and I will listen to you. And you will seek Me and find Me, when you search for Me with all your heart." (Jeremiah 29:12-13) When we ask, seek, and knock, the Bible promises that God will open the door. God will reveal himself to those who seek Him humbly and wholeheartedly.

Expect God to speak to you. Through Christ, and the power of the Holy Spirit, God wants to speak to you on a one-on-one basis, every day. When you receive the fullness of the Holy Spirit, hearing God's voice becomes a natural way of life. The Bible tells us the Father will give His Spirit to all who seek Him. (Luke 11:13) The Holy Spirit will help you understand the Bible so you will know how to apply it to your life. As Christians, we each have the ability to hear from God and be led daily by the Holy Spirit.

God wants to lead us to all the good things He has in store for us. He loves us and wants to be involved in even the smallest details of our lives. John 3:16 is an incredible reminder of God's love for us, "For God so loved the world that He gave His only Son, so that everyone who believes in Him may not perish but may have eternal life." No matter how silent He seems, His love is incredible and it never ends, even when we can't discern His voice. God's Word tells us to acknowledge Him in all our ways, and He will direct our paths. (Proverbs 3:6) When we acknowledge God, we acknowledge that we care what He is thinking. When we trust God, we accept His love and walk in surrendered obedience with Him.

God is constantly speaking to us and giving us direction. It's never God who is not speaking, but it's us who are not hearing. Believe that God is already speaking to you and start listening. Look for His voice and you will find it throughout your day in the form of a gentle nudging or a reminder, from someone He places on your path. He speaks to us through His word, people, signs, symbols, and so much more. When we look for Him, we will find Him everywhere. He is always with us!

Reflect:

How do you hear His voice? What is He saying to You? When you can't hear Him, what do you do?

Pray:

Heavenly Father, I want to hear Your voice. Give me ears to hear You when I pray. Help me learn to listen for Your voice throughout the day. May I always hear the sound of Your voice over the noise of this world. In Jesus' name, I pray. Amen.

Declare:

I believe God is always speaking to me. I humbly and earnestly listen for His voice.

I am thankful for...

_____

_____

_____

_____

_____

Prayer Requests...

_____

_____

_____

_____

_____

What is God's Word saying to you today?...

_____

_____

_____

_____

_____

He Knows What Is Best for Me

"Though you have made me see troubles, many and bitter, you will restore my life again; from the depths of the earth you will again bring me up." - Psalm 71:20

He has me in this place on purpose. Wherever He places me, He does so to strengthen my faith and draw me into a closer relationship with Him. Wherever I am in life, my soul will prosper when I choose to keep Him at the center. When I'm in an uncomfortable place, it is a place of preparation. In this place of preparation, I'm learning to trust Him completely. It is through my struggles that I am being trained to help others who are facing similar struggles. When I learn to endure temptation and choose Him, His grace is magnified and my own character matures.

Reflect:

How are you trusting that God knows what is best for you in this very moment?

Pray:

Heavenly Father, I trust that in this very moment, You have me exactly where you want me. I will seek You each day as I walk this path with You. I ask that You guard my heart and give me the right words at the right time to speak Your truth in love. I ask that you direct my steps so that I may enter the narrow gate that You have prepared for me. In Jesus' name, I pray. Amen.

Declare:

I trust my place in life right now because I trust God knows what is best for me and He is directing my path.

I am thankful for...

_____

_____

_____

_____

_____

Prayer Requests...

_____

_____

_____

_____

_____

What is God's Word saying to you today?...

_____

_____

_____

_____

_____

_____

It Comes from Within

"Whoever believes in me, as Scripture has said, rivers of living water will flow from within them." - John 7:38

The earnest invitation to come and drink of the living water continues to be offered today, to whoever will come. It is in Him, alone, that we receive new life. He is our strength, our song, and our salvation. From Him flow rivers of living water. This living water is given to all who trust in Jesus and His sacrifice on the cross. As the scripture in this message says, 'He who believes on Me, from his innermost being will flow rivers of living water.'

Reflect:

What does this piece of scripture mean to you?

Pray:

Heavenly Father, I believe in You and therefore I believe I have living water flowing within me. Thank you for this beautiful reminder that I am powerful beyond measure in and through You. May I go forth with the courage and conviction to do Your will, Your way, with my faith. In Jesus' name, I pray. Amen.

Declare:

I believe His living water flows within me.

I am thankful for...

_____

_____

_____

_____

_____

Prayer Requests...

_____

_____

_____

_____

_____

What is God's Word saying to you today?...

_____

_____

_____

_____

_____

_____

Be Filled with the Spirit

"Do not get drunk on wine, which leads to debauchery. Instead, be filled with the Spirit, speaking to one another with psalms, hymns, and songs from the Spirit. Sing and make music from your heart to the Lord, always giving thanks to God the Father for everything, in the name of our Lord Jesus Christ." - Ephesians 5:18-20

This is a verse that I have referred to often as I released my wine drinking habit. I took this verse quite literally. I am not supposed to be getting drunk on wine. There was a time in my life that I drank regularly and heavily. When I did make choices outside of God's will, I found that alcohol was the common denominator. Thankfully, God spoke to me and took the taste for wine away as I asked for Him to deliver me from it. Now I choose to be filled with the Holy Spirit and drink mainly cleansing water, tea...and coffee. I enjoy life in a much more meaningful way when I choose to lean wholeheartedly into the love of Jesus. As I turn to Him, I am filled with the Spirit and experience a deeper level of joy and peace that is centered in Christ.

Reflect:

How does this verse speak to you? Do you need God to deliver you from something?

Pray:

Heavenly Father, as I remember all of the good things that You have brought me through, I am reminded that you will do it again. Thank you for taking me to higher ground with You. Help me to learn to walk with You more gracefully as I place my trust in You and surrender completely to Your will. In Jesus' name, I pray. Amen.

Declare:

I am filled with the Spirit.

I am thankful for...

_____

_____

_____

_____

_____

Prayer Requests...

_____

_____

_____

_____

_____

What is God's Word saying to you today?...

_____

_____

_____

_____

_____

Be Rooted and Established in Love

"I pray that out of his glorious riches He may strengthen you with power through His Spirit in your inner being, so that Christ may dwell in your hearts through faith. And I pray that you, being rooted and established in love, may have power, together with all the Lord's holy people, to grasp how wide and long and high and deep is the love of Christ, and to know this love that surpasses knowledge—that you may be filled to the measure of all the fullness of God." - Ephesians 3:16-19

Be rooted and established in love. The Bible states that God is love and that Jesus is God, therefore Jesus is love. He gives us meaning in this life. Love becomes the whole purpose of our life when we are born again and in Christ. Being rooted in love will keep us away from sin and on the right path with God. Love is what causes us to turn from sin. Love is what causes us to tell another person about Jesus. Love is what causes us to forgive, have mercy, show grace, and be patient. God's love is what begins to define our identity. It gives us an eternal purpose and value. As believers, we must look at what we are rooted and established in. Our core identity must be rooted and established in Jesus's love. His love is what should determine our every action, thought, motive, and word. Being rooted in love will keep us from sin and on the right path with God. It will make us more like Jesus every day.

Reflect:

Who or what are you rooted in today? Are you rooted in Jesus or the things of this world?

Pray:

Heavenly Father, I want to be rooted and established in Your love. Help me grow in this area as I face this new challenge in my own love walk today. In Jesus' name, I pray. Amen.

Declare:

I am rooted and established in God's love, therefore I am love.

I am thankful for...

_____

_____

_____

_____

_____

Prayer Requests...

_____

_____

_____

_____

What is God's Word saying to you today?...

_____

_____

_____

_____

_____

_____

Mess to Masterpiece

"And we know that in all things God works for the good of those who love Him, who have been called according to His purpose." - Romans 8:28

The darkness in our lives can become a beautiful backdrop for His radiant light. He can use our mess to create a masterpiece if we let Him. God will take our brokenness and make something beautiful. Some of the greatest musicians have created their best songs from experiences that are rooted in deep sadness and pain. It is in the painful pressing process that we discover our highest purpose.

Reflect:

What is something beautiful that God is creating from your ashes, or your pit of pain? How is He taking your mess and working it together for good?

Pray:

Heavenly Father, I trust You are with me in this very moment and I thank You for that. I don't understand now what You are doing, but I know someday I will. Help me stay in faith and centered in You in the midst of this trial. Help me truly believe that You are taking my mess and working it together to create Your masterpiece. Help me to do exactly what You want me to do, Lord, each moment of each day. When I'm walking in the darkness and can't see the way, help me to trust and know that You are taking my hand and leading me through the darkness into Your glorious light. In Jesus' name, I pray. Amen.

Declare:

I am God's masterpiece.

I am thankful for...

_____

_____

_____

_____

_____

Prayer Requests...

_____

_____

_____

_____

_____

What is God's Word saying to you today?...

_____

_____

_____

_____

_____

_____

Wait on Him

"Blessed is the one who waits." - Daniel 12:12

Waiting may seem easy, but when we are waiting on God to fulfill the desires of our hearts, it is not. We must go through the process of waiting to develop our faith and discipline in Him. When we are in a season of preparation and waiting, it is important to remain in faith, prayer, and thankful patience. He will come at the right time when we believe and keep our heart fixed on Him. He will bless us and equip us to bless others.

Reflect:

How are you waiting? What do you do to maintain peace and joy while you wait?

Pray:

Heavenly Father, I am waiting on You to do what only You can do. As I wait, I will keep my eyes and ears fixed on You. I need You every moment of every day. Lord, I will look for Your presence and listen for Your voice. Lead me. I am Yours. In Jesus' name, I pray. Amen.

Declare:

I am surrendered, thankful, patient, and obedient as I wait on the Lord.

I am thankful for...

_____

_____

_____

_____

_____

Prayer Requests...

_____

_____

_____

_____

_____

What is God's Word saying to you today?...

_____

_____

_____

_____

_____

_____

Look Out for Others

"Look out...for the interests of others." - Philippians 2:4

Spend your time looking out for the interests of others. We need to live our lives less for ourselves and more for others. I have found that when life is really hard, we tend to become closed off and lose our focus. When this happens, it is best to remain open and loving by getting out and doing good for others. In doing good for others, we are also doing good for ourselves. By lifting others, we lift ourselves. In loving others, we love ourselves.

Reflect:

What can you intentionally do this week to look out for the interests of others?

Pray:

Heavenly Father, I am committed to looking out for others in the way that You look out for me. Regardless of what's happening in my life, I want to be the living expression of Your truth and love to all who cross my path. Thank you for giving me the strength to move forward each day. Help me to see the good I can do for others. In Jesus' name, I pray. Amen.

Declare:

I am guided by the Holy Spirit to look out for the interests of others.

I am thankful for...

_____

_____

_____

_____

_____

Prayer Requests...

_____

_____

_____

_____

_____

What is God's Word saying to you today?...

_____

_____

_____

_____

_____

_____

He Lives in You

"You will receive power when the Holy Spirit comes on you."
- Acts 1:8

"My head shall be lifted up above the enemies around me."
- Psalm 27:6

We must invite God to be involved in everything we do. Ask God to fill you with His spirit so that everything you do will be done through His power. Seek Him first and all that you need and desire will be added to your life. He is the giver of every good and perfect gift. Always remember, even when it doesn't feel like it, His power works best in our weakness.

Reflect:

In what ways do you acknowledge His spirit living in you? How can you rest in Him and let His presence flow more freely?

Pray:

Heavenly Father, I know that Your power is made perfect in my weakness. I ask that You go to work within me. May Your spirit flow gracefully through me as I move about my day. I want to experience being in Your presence and sharing Your love and light with others. In Jesus' name, I pray. Amen.

Declare:

Jesus lives in me and His spirit flows effortlessly through me.

I am thankful for...

_____

_____

_____

_____

_____

Prayer Requests...

_____

_____

_____

_____

_____

What is God's Word saying to you today?...

_____

_____

_____

_____

_____

_____

Feed Your Faith

Feed your faith by reading scripture daily. Seek Him above all else and you will starve your fears, anxiety, and worry. When you feed your faith, you can withstand the storm.

"Trust in the Lord and do good; so you will live in the land, and enjoy security. Take delight in the Lord and He will give you the desires of your heart. Commit your way to the Lord; trust in Him, and He will act. Be still before the Lord, and wait patiently for Him." - Psalm 37:3-5

Regardless of what is currently going on in my life, the joy of the Lord is my strength and portion. He fills me with His spirit so that I can do what He has prepared for me to do each day.

"Cast all your anxiety on Him, because He cares for you. Discipline yourselves, keep alert. Like a roaring lion your adversary the devil prowls around, looking for someone to devour. Resist him, steadfast in your faith...and after you have suffered for a little while, the God of all grace, who has called you to His eternal glory in Christ, will Himself restore, support, strengthen, and establish you." - 1 Peter 5:7-10

When your faith is fed daily, the enemy can't control you.

Reflect:

What do you do to feed your faith daily? How do you resist the urge to turn away from God when life is hard?

Pray:

Heavenly Father, I know that I need to feed my faith daily. Regardless of how I feed my faith, I know I need to do it daily. Thank you for giving me the wisdom to know that I need to do this. Help me continue to feed my faith regardless of how I feel. Help me to always choose You and trust You over what I see or feel. In Jesus' name, I pray. Amen.

Declare:

I feed my faith daily.

I am thankful for...

_____

_____

_____

_____

_____

Prayer Requests...

_____

_____

_____

_____

_____

What is God's Word saying to you today?...

_____

_____

_____

_____

_____

_____

Trials Develop Us

"The God of all grace, who called you to His eternal glory in Christ, after you have suffered a little while, will Himself restore you and make you strong, firm, and steadfast."
- 1 Peter 5:10

The trials of life come to develop us. They come to build up our character. A direct blow outwardly can become the greatest blessing inwardly. If God allows anything difficult in our lives, we can be sure that the best way to move through it is with Him. God knows if we are ready for the trial we currently face. We withstand the test of the trial by standing with Him.

Reflect:

How is this latest trial developing you? Are you withstanding the test of the trial by standing with Him? How can you trust God and turn to Him even more in the midst of this trial?

Pray:

Heavenly Father, in the midst of this incredibly difficult trial, I trust You. I consider it pure joy because I know that in the process of what I'm facing, You are developing my character. I know that the victory ultimately belongs to You. Thank you for choosing me as Your vessel to represent You. Give me strength to keep my eyes on You, especially when my heart feels bruised and broken. Please take the broken pieces of my heart and fill them with Your incredible light. In Jesus' name, I pray. Amen.

Declare:

I am being developed by God to be more like Christ.

I am thankful for...

_____

_____

_____

_____

_____

Prayer Requests...

_____

_____

_____

_____

_____

What is God's Word saying to you today?...

_____

_____

_____

_____

_____

_____

He Is My Steadfast Companion

"Draw near to God and He will draw near to you." - James 4:8

When we draw near to God and thank Him in all things, He will light our path through the darkest days. When we have Him as our companion, we have joy and peace in our hearts, because we feel His radiant light shining in and around us as a protective barrier of strength and love.

God is working on the inside of you right now. Trust the process. Trust Him. He is your steadfast companion who will never leave you, nor forsake you.

Reflect:

How are you drawing near to God? Do you make time for Him each day?

Pray:

Heavenly Father, I draw near to You as my steadfast companion because I need You to guide and protect me. When I don't seek You, I make decisions that are outside of Your will for my life. Help me to see the truth and experience the goodness of Your love during the times where I struggle to see through the darkness. In Jesus' name, I pray. Amen.

Declare:

I draw near to God and He draws near to me.

I am thankful for...

_____

_____

_____

_____

_____

Prayer Requests...

_____

_____

_____

_____

What is God's Word saying to you today?...

_____

_____

_____

_____

_____

_____

He Showers Abundant Blessings upon Me

"He has shown you, O mortal, what is good. And what does the Lord require of you? To act justly and to love mercy and to walk humbly with your God." - Micah 6:8

We receive God's mercy and abundant blessings when we, ourselves, give His mercy and blessings to others. We reap what we sow, both good and bad. May we intentionally choose to sow good, godly, seeds of love and kindness as we go about our day. If we want more love, we need to give more love. If we want more compassion, we must give more compassion. We will be showered with abundant blessings when we choose to live righteously. May today be the day that we are intentional about choosing to act justly, love mercy and walk humbly with our God.

Reflect:

Are you glorifying God by how I treat others? How can you show mercy and bless others today?

Pray:

Heavenly Father, each time I receive one of Your gifts, I want to get in the habit of thanking You in that very moment. I know that it is You that showers me with blessings because every good and perfect gift comes from You. In Jesus' name, I pray. Amen.

Declare:

I glorify God by how I treat others. I bless others, and by doing so, receive His abundant blessings in return.

I am thankful for...

_____

_____

_____

_____

_____

Prayer Requests...

_____

_____

_____

_____

What is God's Word saying to you today?...

_____

_____

_____

_____

_____

Wisdom Without Hypocrisy

"If any of you lacks wisdom, you should ask God, Who gives generously to all without finding fault, and it will be given to you." - James 1:5

"The wisdom that comes from heaven is first of all pure; then peace-loving, considerate, submissive, full of mercy and good fruit, impartial and sincere." - James 3:17

True wisdom comes from God. The enemy provides confusion and God provides clarity. We can find out everything that we need to know by asking God and waiting for Him to answer. He answers in His time and in His way. When we pay attention and listen for the whisper of His voice, He will provide the clarity and wisdom that we seek.

Reflect:

Is there an area in your life where you are seeking clarity and wisdom? Are you asking God for wisdom? What are you doing to listen for His voice?

Pray:

Heavenly Father, I trust that You will provide the clarity that I need at just the right time. I know that I need to seek wisdom from You and not from people. Thank you for being with me and leading me through the confusion and heartache. I need You to continue to take my hand and lead me to higher ground. I want Your will to be done in my life. In Jesus' name, I pray. Amen.

Declare:

I receive wisdom from God. He directs my steps.

I am thankful for...

_____

_____

_____

_____

_____

Prayer Requests...

_____

_____

_____

_____

_____

What is God's Word saying to you today?...

_____

_____

_____

_____

_____

_____

He Will Provide

"Commit to the Lord whatever you do, and he will establish your plans." - Proverbs 16:3

"For I know the plans I have for you," declares the Lord, "plans to prosper you and not to harm you, plans to give you hope and a future. Then you will call on me and come and pray to me, and I will listen to you. You will seek me and find me when you seek me with all your heart. I will be found by you," declares the Lord, "and will bring you back from captivity. I will gather you from all the nations and places where I have banished you," declares the Lord, "and will bring you back to the place from which I carried you into exile." - Jeremiah 29:11-14

Consider it all joy. He's purifying and perfecting your heart. Those of us who are facing difficult situations today can take comfort in Jeremiah 29:11, knowing that it is not a promise to immediately rescue us from hardship or suffering, but rather a promise that God has a good plan for our lives. Regardless of our current situation, He will work through it to prosper us and give us a hope and a future.

Reflect:

Are you committing your ways to the Lord? Are you trusting Him to work everything out for your good?

Pray:

Heavenly Father, I believe that You will prosper me and have good plans for my future. Help me to stay close to You so that I can receive every good and perfect gift that You have for me. When my heart is hurting because I don't understand, help me rest in You, with unwavering trust that You will provide. Help me guard my heart against the enemy and keep it pure and open to every good thing You send my way. In Jesus' name, I pray. Amen.

Declare:

I commit everything I do to the Lord and trust Him to give me a good life.

I am thankful for...

_____

_____

_____

_____

_____

Prayer Requests...

_____

_____

_____

_____

_____

What is God's Word saying to you today?...

_____

_____

_____

_____

_____

_____

Be More Like Jesus

"Consider Him who endured such opposition from sinners, so that you will not grow weary and lose heart." - Hebrews 12:3

Lord, teach me to be more like Jesus. I want to be the one who stands tall when others flee. I want to be the one who stays when others walk away. I want to be the one who forgives, especially when it's hard. I want to be the one who shows grace, when others are casting stones. I want to be the one that shows love, even when I'm betrayed. I want to be more like You, Jesus, and less like me.

Reflect:

How is what you're currently facing giving you the opportunity to be more like Jesus? Are you choosing His ways or your own?

Pray:

Heavenly Father, I want to be more like You and less like me. I need Your help to make this happen, because on my own, I am weak. Give me the strength to walk in Your ways each day. When my heart is breaking, please comfort me with Your peace. I need You to show me the way to Your truth and light. Help me respond in love, gentleness, and patience to hurtful behavior. In Jesus' name, I pray. Amen.

Declare:

I am becoming more like Jesus every day.

I am thankful for...

_____

_____

_____

_____

_____

Prayer Requests...

_____

_____

_____

_____

_____

What is God's Word saying to you today?...

_____

_____

_____

_____

_____

_____

Put God First

"Your word is a lamp for my feet, a light on my path."
- Psalm 119:105

If we simply put God first, He adds everything we need to our life according to His perfect plan for us. He lights our path, especially when it's dark and we are walking it alone. When times are hard and lonely on the path, trust that those are times that He is closest to You. Seek His face. Call out to Him. He is at work in your life even when you can't see or feel it. Continue to lean on Him and put Him first in all you do.

Reflect:

In order for His Word to be a lamp for your feet and a light on your path, you need to be reading His word daily. How are you making time to be in the Word every day? How are you putting God first?

Pray:

Heavenly Father, I am so grateful that You direct my path and light it up when it is so dark. I thank You for growing my faith as I put You first in all that I say and do. Thank you for making me strong where I am weak. Help me to always, earnestly, look to You first and remain steadfast in You. In Jesus' name, I pray. Amen.

Declare:

I choose to put God first in my life.

I am thankful for...

_____

_____

_____

_____

_____

Prayer Requests...

_____

_____

_____

_____

_____

What is God's Word saying to you today?...

_____

_____

_____

_____

_____

_____

Build Others up

"Do not let any unwholesome talk come out of your mouths, but only what is helpful for building others up according to their needs, that it may benefit those who listen."
- Ephesians 4:29

Build others up with the words you speak. Only use words that add value and lift others up. Speak life into everyone around you. Leave people better than you found them. Your words have the power to change a life, for better or worse. Speak words that are truthful, kind and encouraging.

Reflect:

How are you intentionally using your words to edify and build others up?

Pray:

Heavenly Father, help me grow in speaking Your truth in love in every opportunity You give me to be a vessel for You. When they see and hear me, let them see and hear You. In Jesus' name, I pray. Amen.

Declare:

I build others up with the words I speak.

I am thankful for...

_____

_____

_____

_____

_____

Prayer Requests...

_____

_____

_____

_____

_____

What is God's Word saying to you today?...

_____

_____

_____

_____

_____

_____

Wash Your Face

"Go, wash yourself seven times in the Jordan, and your flesh will be restored and you will be cleansed." - 2 Kings 5:10

If you want to receive healing and wholeness, you will have to wash the mess of the past off of your face. The healing process is a messy and muddy process, just as it was for Naaman. It often takes time. As the saying goes, we may fall down seven times and have to get back up eight. We have to decide to do the work and understand that healing is almost always a messy, painful, and exhausting process, one that does not provide a direct path or a quick fix.

Lord, no matter how long or messy the journey is, I choose to move forward to healing and wholeness in and through You. I choose to be Your image bearer.

Reflect:

How do we heal when we don't even realize how broken we truly are? Do you lean into the healing process or do you try to avoid it?

Pray:

Heavenly Father, I trust that the only path to healing and wholeness is through You. May I continue to turn to You each day as You work on healing my heart. Create a wholeness in me that I, in my own strength, never knew was possible. Thank you for loving me through my brokenness, into healing and wholeness. In Jesus' name, I pray. Amen.

Declare:

I am healed, whole, restored, and cleansed.

I am thankful for...

_____

_____

_____

_____

_____

Prayer Requests...

_____

_____

_____

_____

_____

What is God's Word saying to you today?...

_____

_____

_____

_____

_____

_____

Time with Him

"Devote yourself to prayer, being watchful and thankful."
- Colossians 4:2

When we spend time with Him, He is training us to think His thoughts. As we spend time with Him, His thoughts begin to form in our minds. His spirit, which lives in us, directs this process. When we spend time with Him, we are strengthened and prepared to face whatever comes our way. Through our sacrifice of our time and devotion, He blesses us far more than we can imagine. When we place Him first, we are in the perfect place to receive His abundant blessings and favor in our lives. The one thing we need right now, more than anything else, is to spend time alone with God.

Reflect:

How do you fit God into your busy life? How often do you spend time alone with Him?

Pray:

Heavenly Father, time with You is the best way I can spend my time. I admit, I don't always want alone time with You, but I know that I need it. Thank you for loving me the way You do. Help me to stay centered in Your love as I go through the changing seasons in life. In Jesus' name, I pray. Amen.

Declare:

I am committed to spending time every day with God.

I am thankful for...

_____

_____

_____

_____

_____

Prayer Requests...

_____

_____

_____

_____

_____

What is God's Word saying to you today?...

_____

_____

_____

_____

_____

_____

A Fierce Storm Will Transform

"So walk in Him rooted and built up in Him." - Colossians 2:6-7

The people who survive the storms and can remain calm in the midst of the storm, are those with deep roots in Christ. Their faith serves as an anchor, helping guide them to peaceful waters. They can draw upon their knowledge of the Word to give them strength to withstand the attacks they may face. Make sure you are prepared for the storm by being firmly planted in Christ, so you may be rooted and built up in Him. May your faith rise above any fear in order to be transformed during life's fierce storm.

Reflect:

How are you feeding your faith? How are you making sure you are rooted and built up in Him?

Pray:

Heavenly Father, as I look back over my path with You, I can see how You have provided me opportunities to take my faith deeper as each new storm arrives. I am rooted more deeply in You with each passing day, therefore the storm doesn't do as much damage as it did before. If anything, the storm causes me to take even deeper roots in You. Thank you for planting me firmly on Your solid ground. In Jesus' name, I pray. Amen.

Declare:

I am deeply rooted in Christ. I am transformed by life's storms to be more like Jesus.

I am thankful for...

_____

_____

_____

_____

_____

Prayer Requests...

_____

_____

_____

_____

_____

What is God's Word saying to you today?...

_____

_____

_____

_____

_____

_____

Walk in Peace

"Turn from evil and do good; seek peace and pursue it."
- Psalm 34:14

We need to walk away from evil and sin in order to walk in peace. Be a peacemaker. When we are being attacked by the enemy, we are to remain constant and fearless, not being frightened at all. (Philippians 1:28) This lets the enemy know how big our God is, for greater is He who is in us than he who is in the world. (1 John 4:4) When we keep our eyes fixed on God, trusting in Him, He will take care of us so that we may walk in peace.

Reflect:

How are you walking in peace today, both inwardly and outwardly?

Pray:

Heavenly Father, I know that in order to walk in peace, I need to be at peace within. I need Your help to experience a peace that surpasses all understanding. Help me to trust You so that I may experience Your peace and walk boldly in it today. In Jesus' name, I pray. Amen.

Declare:

I seek, receive, and walk in His peace.

I am thankful for...

_____

_____

_____

_____

_____

Prayer Requests...

_____

_____

_____

_____

_____

What is God's Word saying to you today?...

_____

_____

_____

_____

_____

_____

Be Fiercely Authentic

"For God has not given us a spirit of fear, but of power and of love and of a sound mind." - 2 Timothy 1:7

I have found that while we tend to crave authenticity, it takes real strength and courage to live authentically without retreating to the walls of safety we've built within. Not everyone is ready to own their truth. Keep being fiercely authentic anyway. We need to see more people being brave in owning who they truly are, and not some watered down version of who others think they are. People will judge you anyway. Let them judge the real you. When you are brave, you inspire others to be brave too!

Reflect:

How are you living authentically? Are there areas in your life where you aren't being your most authentic self?

Pray:

Heavenly Father, I want to be fiercely authentic in who You created me to be. Help me live my life with passion and purpose. Help me to honor You in the way that I live my life. May others be set free by seeing me live in complete authenticity. In Jesus' name, I pray. Amen.

Declare:

I am fearfully and wonderfully made. I am fiercely authentic in who I am and how I live, to honor and glorify Christ.

I am thankful for...

_____

_____

_____

_____

_____

Prayer Requests...

_____

_____

_____

_____

What is God's Word saying to you today?...

_____

_____

_____

_____

_____

Take the Next Step

"Whoever serves me must follow me; and where I am, my servant also will be. My father will honor the one who serves me." - John 12:26

Take the next courageous step in faith. In order to follow Him wholeheartedly, you must be willing to take risks. Let Him lead you step by step through this day. Keep your eyes fixed on Him and He will give you exactly what you need when you need it. Relax into His loving presence, for "even though you walk through the valley of the shadow of death, you will fear no evil, for you are with Him." (Psalm 23:4)

Reflect:

What courageous next step do you need to take in faith?

Pray:

Heavenly Father, I know I need to keep seeking Your will for my life. I feel stuck at times, not knowing where You are taking me. Please release me from my need to know, so that I may follow You with confidence. In Jesus' name, I pray. Amen.

Declare:

I am courageous in my walk with the Lord.

I am thankful for...

_____

_____

_____

_____

_____

Prayer Requests...

_____

_____

_____

_____

_____

What is God's Word saying to you today?...

_____

_____

_____

_____

_____

_____

Trials Are Necessary

"Consider it pure joy, my brothers, whenever you face trials of many kinds." - James 1:2

Proverbs 3:15 says, "She is more precious than jewels; nothing you desire compares with her." A jewel needs to be polished and with the polishing comes friction. If we are to be considered more precious than jewels, then we must be ready to be polished. In the process, we will experience friction in the form of trials that refine our most authentic shimmer; a shimmer that represents and reflects the image of Christ.

Reflect:

In the midst of your trial, are you surrendered to the process? Are you able to push past the pain and consider it pure joy? How are you willfully submitting to God as He polishes you?

Pray:

Heavenly Father, in the midst of my pain and lack of understanding, I am doing my best to look to You and trust that this trial has a divine purpose. Help me push past my feelings so that I may remain surrendered to You as You polish and perfect me to be Your beautiful image bearer. In Jesus' name, I pray. Amen.

Declare:

I am being polished by God to be His beautiful image bearer.

I am thankful for...

_____

_____

_____

_____

_____

Prayer Requests...

_____

_____

_____

_____

_____

What is God's Word saying to you today?...

_____

_____

_____

_____

_____

_____

You Have Found Favor

"But the angel said to her, 'Do not be afraid, Mary; you have found favor with God.'" - Luke 1:30

Be genuine. Be giving. Be kind. Have faith. Walk in humility, truth, and love.

Love God with all your heart. Without loving Him, we cannot expect to gain His favor. Love people. If you want God's favor, then start caring more for people. As we take a stand for God and His causes, His favor is released upon us.

Be a genuine, unconditional giver. Give with godly motives. Seeking God first and walking faithfully with Him throughout the day also leads to His favor. "Seek first the Kingdom of God and His righteousness and all these things will be added unto you." (Matthew 6:33)

Being humble and submitting to God by resisting the need to take matters into our own hands is an ingredient to receiving His favor. Humility and confidence in God will win His blessings and favor. Humility leads to favor for not only yourself, but all those around you. Through humility, let's create an atmosphere of favor in our lives that can overflow to others. "God resists the proud, but gives grace to the humble." (1 Peter 5:5)

Be honest in all you say and do. "The Lord detests dishonest scales, but accurate weights find favor with Him." (Proverbs 11:1) Wisdom leads to favor. If any of us lacks wisdom (which all of us do), we need to seek it from God, not people. (James 1:5)

When we find God, we find His favor. How do we find Him? We need to earnestly seek Him and that is exactly where He is found. He is with us at all times. All we need to do is turn and seek His face. "For those who find me find life and receive favor from the Lord." (Proverbs 8:35)

Reflect:

What are you doing for His kingdom? What are you doing for others? Have you found His favor? What is one area you can grow in, from those listed above?

Pray:

Heavenly Father, thank you for the favor that You have bestowed upon my life. I have found favor with You by seeking You first and walking with You throughout the day. Help me stay centered in You, giving the enemy no room to instill worry or fear when I face new challenges. In Jesus' name, I pray. Amen.

Declare:

I am blessed and highly favored.

I am thankful for...

_____

_____

_____

_____

_____

Prayer Requests...

_____

_____

_____

_____

_____

What is God's Word saying to you today?...

_____

_____

_____

_____

_____

_____

Choose Faith

"Now faith is confidence in what we hope for and assurance about what we do not see." - Hebrews 11:1

To choose faith in the midst of fear, we must know God's word. His Word is the foundation and the beginning of choosing faith over fear. Our knowledge of the Bible is a major factor in the strength or weakness of our faith. Knowing what God's word says gives us the courage to boldly walk in faith, trusting Him for the impossible.

We must commit ourselves to not only know God's word, but to obey it. Our practice of obeying God's word gives us confidence when we are confronted by fear. Faith is energizing when we put God's word into action. The more we step out in faith by walking in obedience to the word of God with a pure heart, the more our faith grows in Him and the less fearful we become of things that we don't understand.

Reflect:

How are you choosing faith over fear? How are you choosing faith in the midst of uncertainty?

Pray:

Heavenly Father, I want my faith to be so strong that fear doesn't even think to knock on my door. May I be so armored up in Your truth that fear is quickly shut down when it shows up in my life. Thank you for giving me a spirit of courage and strength. Help me to grow my faith in You so that I can see clearly with Your eyes when times appear dark and uncertain. In Jesus' name, I pray. Amen.

Declare:

I have the vision of Christ as I exercise my faith in Him.

I am thankful for...

_____

_____

_____

_____

_____

Prayer Requests...

_____

_____

_____

_____

_____

What is God's Word saying to you today?...

_____

_____

_____

_____

_____

_____

Say His Name, Speak His Word

"Jesus. Jesus. You make the darkness tremble…"

There are times we need to speak, boldly, out loud what the Bible teaches. Fear breeds on our doubts in the silence of our thoughts. Yet, in contrast, our faith is strengthened and grows out of our spoken confidence of God's truth. There's something about reading, speaking, and meditating on scripture that helps us to push forward when we want to give up. We need to speak His word within and out loud to bolster our faith and silence our fears.

I am the righteousness of God in Christ. When I say the name of Jesus, the enemy flees.

Jesus changes us

By faith, we are made whole. We must be open to receiving daily the fullness of healing that Jesus died to give us. We do this by submitting to the power of the Holy Spirit who is at work within us. When we focus on Jesus, everything else falls into its proper place.

Let God transform you into a new person by changing the way you think.

Who are you when you're at your very best? What are you going to do to step into your authentic purpose?

You have a unique fingerprint to leave a lasting impact. You have a divine purpose to fulfill.

God sees our hearts and He wants us to see one another's hearts. We block that when we lack authenticity. Be fiercely, unapologetically, authentically you, the 'you' that He created in His image.

Love Like Jesus

To love like Jesus, we must do so on purpose and with intention. If we seek opportunities to love people, we will find them. Live out the love of God by choosing to be the hands, eyes, and feet of Jesus.

To be the change we wish to see in the world, we need more people getting out into the world with the intention to live and love like Jesus.

Jesus, help us to live and love like You.

Acknowledgements

I would like to thank God for the courage and strength that He provides in my weakest moments.

I would like to thank my family for their unwavering support, especially when it comes to my passionate love for Jesus. I want to thank my parents, Ian and Judy Fulp, for being such incredible human beings who I look up to and aspire to be more like with each passing day.

I hope my children, Damien Fulp, Patrick McMahon, and Teresa McMahon, will be able to say... "Our mother loved and chased after Jesus with all her heart. She pointed us to Jesus with every chance she got and she loved us with a love that could have only come from God."

I would like to thank Toshiro Morgan for being the first man to come into my life and love Jesus with me. I am thankful for his leadership in our study of the Word and for his earnest choice to glorify God in our relationship. God brought us together at just the right time, so that He could reach a deeper place in my heart. Many of the messages in this devotional are inspired by our walk together in Christ.

I thank You, Jesus, for never leaving nor forsaking me. May Your light continue to shine bright within my heart, so that You may be known to all who come to know me.

This season may be cold and dark, but we must remember that we have His light within to shine before others. (Matthew 5:16)

Mary Teresa Fulp, Alaska 2020

Let His light shine like sunbeams from your eyes.

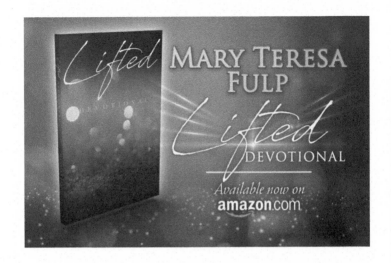

First book published by Mary Teresa Fulp

Lifted Devotional

"Humble yourselves before the Lord and He will lift you up."
- James 4:10

Made in USA - Kendallville, IN
1224753_9780578839837
02.11.2021 2017